WorkJockey

Work Less, Live More, and Be Happy

THOMAS NOBLE
BOOKS

Wilmington, DE

Author Contact: SamSlay.com

Thomas Noble Books
Wilmington, DE
www.thomasnoblebooks.com
Library of Congress Control Number: 2017951762.
ISBN: 978-1-945586-08-8
First Printing: 2017

DEDICATION

To Stephen Alan Slay and Sydney Lauren Slay.
You will always be my greatest success and my greatest adventure.
I will always love you deeper than you can ever imagine.

AND

To Vickie Slay and Carol Sherman, who brought you both
into this world and helped raise you from infants.

In loving memories of my mother, Mary Belle Slay
(9/23/1923 – 4/7/1989), who gave everything she had to
see me succeed in whatever endeavor I pursued. And to my
father, Jackson Lamar "Bill" Slay (12/6/1939 – 3/14/2017),
who always had a tear in his eye when he spoke with me, not
because he was sad or disappointed, but because he was proud
and because he loved me deeply. I did not understand the
tears at the time; however, having two children of my own,
it became abundantly clear where those tears came from – a
very deep and caring love that only a parent can understand
and experience. My mom passed away many years ago and yet
her spirit is with me today. My dad died while I was writing
this book and I am so sorry he will not get to read it and see it
published. Again, I know Mom and Dad would be proud.

TABLE OF CONTENTS

CHAPTER 1

SADDLE UP – TIME TO BECOME A WORKJOCKEY

Make your labor work for you instead of against you.

Too many people are slowly crumbling under the load of trying to blend work and life. They are stressed out, unhappy, and feel trapped by the demands of their jobs but powerless to make changes. While growing up, you might have heard, as I did, "Get a steady job that you can depend on."

In today's economy it can be even more tempting to believe that you are trapped and at the mercy of your employer, even if you enjoy your job. Economic challenges have reinforced the idea that the best way to survive is to put your head down and do whatever it takes to keep your monthly paycheck.

In *WorkJockey*, I want to show you a better way.

I've been where you are – overworked, overtired, and disconnected from my family because I spent every possible moment working. It cost me a marriage. And it took a toll on my health until I started to look at my life and career in a different way.

I became a WorkJockey – someone who is able to jockey my career and do the things that enable me to win a happy and healthy life while maintaining the income I need to support my family. I want to share my experiences with you so that you, too, can stop feeling trapped and start taking control of your life and work.

Be a WorkJockey by working less, living more, accomplishing more, and being happier.

A WorkJockey places life ahead of work. You work to live; you don't live to work. This premise is as applicable to the kind of life you wish to lead today, if not more so, than it was when it was first uttered. You have various needs, desires, goals, and dreams; however, we all share a common aim, and obtaining an income is a necessity for living a normal and prosperous life.

How I Became a WorkJockey

My professional career started in law enforcement, although I had other jobs before that. I worked seven years in uniform, seven years in investigations, and the rest of my time in law enforcement in administration as a sergeant, lieutenant, and four years as a chief of police.

When I retired after twenty-four years in law enforcement I discovered I had never really been a "cop." I was an entrepreneur with a gun and a badge – a WorkJockey who learned over time that I had to manage my career instead of waiting to be promoted or to finally get the salary that would give me the life I wanted. I learned that if I wanted to grow in my profession, I needed to make it happen. No one was going to hand me a great career.

However, I did not learn the WorkJockey lessons until I'd lost my marriage and some of my health. I was stressed out, working many hours of overtime, and pretty miserable. Plus I was getting into trouble at work. I was always trying to improve things. My supervisors were beating me up saying, "Hey, we don't need you to improve anything. We need you to just go out and put somebody in jail. Do your job. Don't worry about all this other stuff you're trying to improve." For a long time I thought, "Dang, is there something wrong with me?"

And then about halfway through my career, I realized that there was actually something wrong with the culture and the system. I realized I had career options and could change myself and my approach to work. I became a WorkJockey and started putting myself and my family first. I worked on my confidence and time management skills, and found that I had more skills than I realized. I made many improvements internally, and they were validated many times by promotions and awards I earned.

For example, I helped take an organization paperless, and helped another organization, the Bay County Sheriff's Office, go digital with some of their photos and video files and take them to another level. It saved them hundreds of thousands of dollars because it was done internally, and I realized, "Maybe I'm not such an idiot after all. Maybe I'm just a young guy in an environment that doesn't look for improvement." My law enforcement career began my path of always looking for better and more efficient ways to do things.

Once I learned the WorkJockey mindset, I grew in every way, personally and professionally. Today I'm happy, doing what I love, and have the health, wealth, and family life I've always dreamed of. It wasn't magic or good luck. Instead, it was a series of changes in my thinking and behavior.

In *WorkJockey* I share the steps I used to take responsibility for my career and my life. These steps are simple, but not always easy. The WorkJockey process takes a common sense approach to personal and career development that anyone can use. You don't need a university degree or a fat bank account. You do need the desire to have a better life and the willingness to make changes.

Work is a tool to get those things you need and want. That is ALL work really is. You don't want to balance work with life; you want a *work/life blend*. You want to LIVE. But how do you get there from where you are today?

Before I get too deep into the specifics of becoming a WorkJockey, I want you to think for just a moment about what you would want if you were LARGE AND IN CHARGE of your future. What is really your ideal lifestyle? I am not talking about pie in the sky. I mean the life you would realistically enjoy, beginning from where you stand right now.

A WorkJockey is someone who lives life on their terms, whatever those unique terms may be. A WorkJockey rides a career like a horse, leading it, guiding it, and jockeying it instead of being at its mercy. They build a life that makes them happy, with work in its proper place. If they have built the right kind of life, there is no worry about work/life balance. WorkJockeys *work less, live more, accomplish more, and are happier*.

If you become a WorkJockey, you'll experience:

- Less stress
- More personal and professional satisfaction
- Happier personal relationships
- Deeper experiences

Sound intriguing? It's possible for everyone, no matter where you are today. I'm going to show you how to shape the life you have into the life you want.

Work/Life BALANCE – creates unremarkable performance.

Work/Life BLEND – creates remarkable performance and a harmonious life.

CHAPTER 2

BEGINNING THE WORKJOCKEY JOURNEY

Be a victor, not a victim!

Becoming a WorkJockey begins with a mental *paradigm shift*. Forget the traditional things you grew up believing for the moment. In time you will be able to evaluate them and either transform them until they parallel your new philosophy, or prove them to be outdated and/or unproductive. Your goal is to place work in the proper perspective.

Why do you work? Work is to provide an income in order to pay your bills and feed your family. Beyond that work can be about personal achievement, self-expression, progress, and creativity.

For a moment let's consider that you are wealthy and money is no longer an issue; you have all the recurring income you need without having to work. What would you do with your newfound freedom, particularly those forty-plus hours a week you are now using for work? What would your life look like? For many this is impossible to imagine. Even those who have earned this status can rarely imagine being without a mission or vision for themselves that doesn't include some labor.

Once you have this vision of your wealthy life, work backwards for a moment. Did you inherit this money, win a lottery, or earn it? Each of these methods of obtaining money provides different experiences and imprints different philosophies in your mind. If you inherited money without having to work for it, you cannot truly appreciate the efforts others go through to reach their level of success. If you were to lose your inheritance, you might find yourself destitute. You might believe that all is lost and you cannot survive in the world that exists around you now. If you won the lottery, your life experience might have been one of working hard and pursuing goals or it might have been one of entitlement, living on the welfare system. Either way you would think very differently about money and wealth.

True wealth comes from the ability to replicate it if it were lost and you had to reacquire it. Becoming a WorkJockey is not about winning the lottery or inheriting wealth. Being a WorkJockey is placing labor or work in its proper perspective for you. Whether you work in fast food, like I once did, or you're a highly paid engineer, this premise applies to you just the same. Your work must be compartmentalized. It should take up the proper amount of time to fit your goals and objectives, and no more.

Work and life have very different goals, and it's best to consider them separately. Even though being flexible requires you to blur the lines from time to time, you should be able to recognize that the goals of work and life are not the same.

I have been affiliated with the non-profit Florida League of Cities since 2014. This organization has a strong focus on internal and external members. They focus and value their members first and then they focus on the delivery of their products and services to members at large. The League established a core set of values known as The 12 FLC [Florida League of Cities] Culture Commitments. More important than just creating the twelve commitments and adopting them, the League provides a recurring mission to train and emphasize these commitments to internal members and future members. The League has been successful at compartmentalizing the mission so that internal members are not overlooked while looking after external members' needs.

The culture of the League was not like any other I had experienced in my working life. They first recognize the individual's contribution and the value of each employee. At the time of writing this book my experiences with other employees of the League have been exemplary. Work in the League is more like working on a team than in any other organization I have been associated with. When I receive a request for help from someone from the League's office, I don't hesitate to provide service. I don't run requests by their supervisor; I offer them service. Whenever I have asked for help or assistance from other League staff they have always been willing to help me. This is a far cry from the mantras of most organizations.

I witnessed a very heart-warming event when a woman in the office, Anita Wick, had a medical emergency with her daughter and literally had to leave the country immediately to rescue her daughter, who was gravely ill and all alone in another country. There was no question the organization would suffer due to Anita's absence. She is a stalwart of motivation and performance. However, the League did not hesitate to provide whatever time off and assistance Anita needed to help her daughter. Anita has returned to work and her daughter is back in the United States, recovering and progressing well.

This is the kind of behavior from an organization that deserves reverence and support as a model for others to follow, no matter whether non-profit or for-profit. Once, at a League organizational retreat, the director, Mike Sittig, said, "We may not be for profit, however – we are not for loss either." Great point. The bills must be paid in order to continue providing products and services to members. The League offers the opportunity for employees to grow and develop while providing their members great products and services.

What's Your Current Category?

Your work can fall into several categories depending on how you view it. You might have a job, a career, a hobby, or a passion. Your vocation can hold more than one meaning for you. Most folks are in a job. I define a job as something that most of us would gladly give up if money were no object. In other words, if you had enough money to live the life you desire, you would quit your job immediately. You would pursue other endeavors that you enjoy.

If you have a career, you would probably think twice before you stop working in that career. Your chosen profession drew you in and gave your work meaning far beyond a paycheck. A career is much harder to walk away from. If you win the lottery, you would have to make a difficult decision before leaving your career behind. Even if the decision is difficult, I believe you would still leave the career behind and pursue other interests. A career has more personal meaning than a job because you chose it for a particular reason and because you're making a contribution to the world at large – or at least to your organization.

A hobby is something you do for enjoyment but not primarily to earn money. A hobby rarely benefits mankind in the long run. You are engaged in a fun activity that no matter what the return on investment, you would likely do anyway. Would you agree that when money is of no real concern, a hobby sounds more appealing?

Now let me move on to career dreams, or passion. Napoleon Hill once said, "A goal is a dream with a deadline." I like that thought. Work should have meaning beyond a paycheck or you're just earning dollars for your time. When your work is your passion, you would do that work for the pleasure of it even if you didn't need the money.

Few of us expect our work to be our passion. Most were taught to get a good, steady job that would support us financially, and search for pleasure outside of work. What if it did not have to be that way? What if you could be so passionate about your work that you looked forward to Monday mornings?

Whether you are in a job you like or one you hate, the right attitude helps your work provide more meaning than merely a paycheck. What does your work provide you? For example, all work provides experience. Work provides self-expression. Work provides an opportunity to grow as an individual as well as an employee. Every job, without exception, offers you these growth opportunities regardless of whether you like or dislike your work.

Your job does not need to be permanent. In fact, trends developing now suggest that workers will have many more jobs in their lifetimes than their parents or relatives had in theirs. Let me be clear: I don't think you should be job hopping on a whim. Never leave a job without a good reason, and certainly not until you have a new job to transfer to. I have seen many people make this mistake, and as a result they became desperate, and rather than getting a better job they got a worse job because they needed the income immediately.

Imagine you have a career that required study and preparation. If you are in the middle of this career you might think it's impossible to change careers. Then a new opportunity presents itself. Is it the opportunity you were hoping for? Even if it is, you should still compartmentalize it to make it work for you. Working is not the only thing you should do in life. Your work should provide for the things you want beyond income, otherwise you are always seeking a *bigger, better deal*. Lewis Carroll wrote, "If you don't know where you are going, any road will take you there." Don't wander your way through life. Try to be specific even if you don't have all the answers now.

Decide to Change

Making a change in your work life is a first step in getting what you want. You might think you are "too busy," and wonder how to find the time to change direction. You find time for everything else you want, and this is no different. If you make your career change a priority, you *will* make it happen.

How do you know if your job is your passion? If you would perform the duties of that job for free, even if you did not need the money, your job is your passion. If you had all the financial resources you needed for you and your family even without the job, you would continue this work. That is how you know you have a passion for the work you do and the manner and place where you do it. Wow, what a great feeling you would have.

Think of the Pope, for example. Although I'm sure he is well taken care of, you would have to agree he has a passion for the work he's doing and knows it is right for him. Follow your skill set, your passion, and your enthusiasm, and make it pay while understanding that you still must place even a passion in its proper role in your life.

In this book you'll learn the steps for becoming a WorkJockey. Here's an overview:

- Identify what type of work you are doing. Is it
  - A job?
  - A career?
  - A passion?
  - A hobby?
- Determine what type of work you prefer to do
  - Manual labor
  - Skilled labor
  - Administrative or management
  - Analytical or research
  - Something else?
- How much time do you wish to spend on this labor?
  - Paid by the hour
  - Paid by the project
  - Paid by the result
  - Paid for time and talent, or value
- Evaluate the following:
  - Why are you working?
  - Are you waiting for something external to happen to or for you?

- ° Does your work interfere with your success, or promote it?
- ° Are you growing, or dying on the work vine?
- ° Have you compartmentalized your work? (Even a passionate pursuit should be compartmentalized.)

Start from where you are in the work cycle right now. Every one of us is in a different place. Unless you have never had a job, you should recognize where you are before you can plan to get where you want to be.

As you read further, I'll give you more information about each area of the WorkJockey path.

Assess Your Personality

Are you someone who gets along well with others? Do you enjoy working with and for others to accomplish goals together, or do you prefer to work alone? Even if your personality has worked for you for years, that's not a strong indicator that you haven't been held back or even hampered in your success by your personality.

Just this past week I was about to teach a class in Face-To-Face Communications. While I was standing near the front of the room one of the attendees walked in and I greeted him with a "Good Morning," to which he did not reply; he even turned away from me. He immediately walked over to one of the workbooks I had placed on a table, opened it, and said, "I don't need any of these stupid games," and he promptly walked out of the room without saying another word. How do you think I perceived this attendee's behavior, and how would others perceive him? Society does not appreciate this type of behavior; we react to it, and not positively. If this were an employee of yours, would you promote him or provide a pay raise? He would likely be skating on thin ice. In fact his supervisor told me, "I think he has to go." And you know what that means. Unfortunately no one had been able to teach him about his personal brand or coach him for success.

Take inventory of not only your skill level but also your ability to follow and to lead. Analyze your strengths and weaknesses. Determine what you do well and what you find interesting and enjoyable. Determining your strengths allows you to accentuate them and minimize your weaknesses. Validate the importance of a weakness before spending time on improving it. Some might advise you to work on your weaknesses, but I think you should upgrade only those weaknesses that improve your skills inventory and move you closer to your ideal purpose and goals. We all have weaknesses. If yours are unimportant to your success, don't waste a lot of time trying to strengthen them. If they must be improved so you can pursue your goals, by all means work on them so they become assets instead of liabilities. I have never been good at algebra, but I seem to be able to compensate in other ways and have never found the need to exhaust additional effort to learn algebra. If you plan to be an engineer, scientist, or doctor, algebra might be necessary. If algebra is not a skill you need, don't waste valuable, irreplaceable time and effort on it.

Assess Your Use of Time

Are you managing your time effectively? Let me take another contrarian viewpoint and tell you that time management is a myth. You can manage resources and obtain more as needed, but you cannot get more time. The clock ticks on, never stops, never slows down, and time cannot be replenished.

What you can do is identify priorities and decide what you will spend your time on. It's surprising how much more you can accomplish with a change in focus. Stop wasting time doing things that do not produce results or doing things that actually waste the valuable resource of time.

I survived without a television from 2004 to 2008. I was cutting costs and realized I needed to cut the cord on this total waste of money and time. I had found myself watching television for two hours at a time, and in the end I did not even enjoy the shows I had watched. It's sad to say that we sometimes waste our time doing things we don't even enjoy.

You might ask what happened in 2008. My older brother Richard Winston moved in with me, so I subscribed to cable television again for his benefit. However, I noticed the four-year hiatus from television had modified my perspective on watching television. I now recognize the difference between distraction, entertainment, and education, and I act accordingly with my television access. In other words, the television is off most of the time. What a change that has made in my life, and I encourage you to make this change as well to make your lifestyle more effective and efficient.

CHAPTER 3

WORKJOCKEY PRINCIPLES

Do you resist change and insist on comfort?

If you want to be a WorkJockey, it's important to examine the principles that guide your life. You were taught principles during your childhood that shaped how you view your life and work. These principles are not wrong, but I ask you to reconsider them so they won't interfere with your future success. For example, you might have been taught that a job is a job so long as you get paid. Working is necessary; that part is true. However, why and how you work is entirely up to you.

To carve out the work life that best suits you, establish a new set of principles and norms. This may be difficult to imagine while you are still living the life you have created up to this point. Yet to become a WorkJockey and live a life that pleases you, it is essential to evaluate your principles and get rid of ones that don't support the life you want.

As you read the principles of a WorkJockey below, your mind might put up a fight and try to convince you that you can't change. But everyone has the ability to change. If you want a better life, be determined and driven to make the turnaround and travel in a new direction.

These WorkJockey principles will guide you:

- Take care of yourself first.
- Spend your time in accordance with your goals.
- Spend your time with supportive and uplifting people.
- Don't spend your time with people who drag you down.
- Value your moments and memories.
- You are your own personal brand, a *Brand of One*.
- Make a good impression with your brand.

Taking care of yourself begins with taking care of your mind. What goes into your mind has a direct affect and impact on you. The more positive things you put into your mind, the more positive you will become. Expose yourself to twice the positive stimuli that you might think necessary, because the negativity in the world around us is more pervasive than the positive. Most folks are more affected and influenced by negative stimulus than by positive stimulus. Flood your mind with the positive to offset and even push out all negative stimuli. Realize that most people are good. Begin with this premise and your transition will be much easier.

Deciding how you will spend your time requires you to become keenly aware of your time. You might consider drafting a log for one week, writing down everything you do. Then categorize it into work, family, personal, and leisure time. Keeping in mind how you actually spent your time that week, modify the time you spend in each category to fit your goals. Only then can you determine what is a waste and what is a priority for you.

What you will do during some of your daily twenty-four hours is predetermined. You should have eight hours of sleep every day. Your body will get this sleep, or it will eventually take it by making you ill. You likely also have to be at work for eight hours. So your discretionary time is limited to eight hours a day (more on the weekends) before you even begin your prioritization.

Let's discuss with whom you will spend your time. It has been said that you become the average of the people you spend your time with. Who does that make you? If you don't like the answer, make some immediate adjustments. Because if you don't begin spending time with people who can support your WorkJockey efforts, you will be fighting a never-ending battle and will be unable to change.

Spending time with uplifting people you admire is critical to your success along your journey. Spend time with folks who share your principles so that they can encourage you to stay grounded in those principles. They do not have to share your goals, just the principles you wish to live by. Do these people support you? Do you trust them to look out for your best interests? Do they like and care about you as a person? These are all important questions to answer if you wish to accelerate rather than to short-circuit your success in life.

Who will you stop spending your time with? Jealously guard your time and limit access to you by those who drag you down or interfere with your pursuits. They might hamper you purposely or inadvertently, but the results are equally detrimental. You are not being selfish; you are simply being guarded. Determine what individuals you meet are seeking and who they are as people. Every minute spent with them either helps or hinders your growth. You only have so much time, and you cannot afford to be arbitrary or benevolent with your time with the wrong people.

Every minute is very important from here forward. I am not suggesting that you should not enjoy your free time. Use your time as you wish, just remember to budget needed time the same way you budget your financial resources. You can always waste a little of your time just as you waste a little cash from time to time.

Your time is most important to you; it's your talent that's important to your employer. Guard your time carefully so you can thrive in your career and have time for your life as well.

The title of this book is *WorkJockey: Work Less, Live More, and Be Happy!* I believe that your work should work for you and not against you. Work should be more than a mere paycheck. Because it takes a large portion of your time and your life, your work should benefit you personally, not just pay your bills. The eight hours you spend at work should contribute to your life pursuits.

Moments and Memories

Life is about moments and memories. I was having a dinner conversation with Ron Peters, the director of the risk control department of the Florida League of Cities. Our discussion ventured into the area of passionate work versus mere employment. I told him that the conversation was a moment that would become a memory of a past experience. I explained further that life is entirely about interactions, and thoughts and feelings about these interactions.

We tend to get tunnel vision and forget some of the most important things we experience. For example, when my daughter Sydney was six years old I was driving down the highway and she was securely fastened and tucked into her car seat. She was playing Leap Frog, a computer game. Unfortunately video games can be a little loud, and particularly distracting when you are driving in traffic. I said, "Sydney, you'll have to turn the volume down so I can hear to drive." Like most kids she responded right away and turned it down… noooot… you know I am kidding – when do kids do what you ask the first time? At the next stoplight I turned around and said with a more authoritative voice, "Baby, you are going to have to either turn the volume down or stop playing your game for now." She cocked her head to the side slightly and said, "Daddy… I'm a kid… I have to have something to do… otherwise it's going to get real crazy up in here." I just chuckled, and when the light changed I drove on. I was amused, shocked even, and did not know what else to say. She got me good.

Since that time I have told that story to many audiences and it never fails to get a good laugh. It's a wonderful memory for me. I even told Sydney about using her comment in my presentations, and you wouldn't believe what this six-year-old said next: "Am I getting paid?" That's my little entrepreneur talking. I told her, "You're going to Disney World again this year, aren't you? …That's your payment." Everything is a negotiation these days.

Good times exist. This is just an example of life's moments, and a memory I would miss if I hadn't paid close attention. "How important are these memories?" you might ask. There is nothing more important than moments and memories. Work will never be more important. Be sure to compartmentalize work into its proper place, and don't miss your moments and memories.

Priorities change throughout your life because you change from day to day and from year to year. So evaluating your time is an ongoing responsibility. Time does not change. You change. You cannot manage time; time manages you in a way, because time remains the only constant, and your priorities are always changing. You get one round in life. It's not like golf where you can play again until you get better. Life is finite. You don't get a mulligan or a do-over. There is wasted time in every job setting and in every organization. If you want to improve how you use your time, begin with your work life.

Recently I assisted two organizations in their efforts to become paperless. Both organizations felt it could not be done. When we reviewed the types of work being completed, we found many examples of work that had no value to the organization or to the employees. Things had simply always been done that way so no one questioned it. These organizations were caught up in busy work and wasting valuable time and resources.

What is the value of your time? You might believe you are worth more than minimum wage, but if you take inventory of your skills and your value in the marketplace, you might find your worth is close to minimum wage. Some folks can clearly articulate their value at greater than minimum wage. And some might greatly underestimate their value. I once read that if you're worth more than ten dollars an hour you should pay someone else to perform low-level tasks so you can spend your time on more valuable tasks for which you are qualified and might be the only one authorized to perform.

What Kind of Person Do You Wish to Become?

Some folks have never given this a second thought. Many of us think we have become the only person we are capable of becoming. We wrongly believe we cannot improve who we are because of the way we grew up. This is simply not true. You can improve who you are. And you can become worse off. These are choices you make, intentionally or unintentionally, based on the principles you wish to live by. Do you want to be an honest, truthful person, willing to help others, or do you prefer to only help yourself at whatever the cost to others?

Most folks believe they are good people. Would your employer and your friends describe you as honest, trustworthy, and a hard worker, or would they describe you in more unflattering terms? Would your co-workers vote to keep you? Answering these questions is hard for some and easy for others.

You are a Brand of One. Every contact with the outside world leaves an impression on others. You want that impression to be a positive one. Strive to create a positive impression and be prepared to offset your mistakes through continued good works. Just as businesses have a brand identity, so do you.

You make a first impression and it sticks. You can only hope most of your first impressions are positive. Your appearance, your voice, your demeanor, and the way you treat others are on display and go into the formula of your first impressions.

Your environment helps create you. This is not an excuse you should use to explain poor behavior; it's merely one of the reasons you are who you are. If your environment is not supportive, you might need to change it. You can change a negative environment, negative relationships, and negative thoughts by flooding your brain with things of a positive nature.

You became who and what you are through the many influences in your life. If you have been doing well and are proud of who you have become, this is great. You have a good brand. You are among a select few. Keep up the good work.

If you are not getting the results you wish for or you are not where you want to be, an about-face may be necessary. Drug addicts often must hit rock bottom before they are motivated make a change. Unfortunately no one person knows where rock bottom is for anyone else. As long as you are in your right mind you can make immediate changes in your environment and behavior. You don't need all the answers in advance to get started. Just get started and your path will become clearer as you travel in a new direction.

Just to recap:

- Your time is the most valuable asset you possess.
- Flood your mind with positive stimuli: books, audios, videos, and movies.
- Track your time to evaluate your use of it.
- Terminate negative, unhealthy relationships.
- Work effectively, efficiently, but *not* excessively.
- Eliminate work beneath your value: delegate, automate, or eliminate.
- Identify your personal brand: honest, trustworthy, consistent with integrity?

If a vote were taken today, would your employer or your employees vote to keep you? Would your friends vote for or against keeping you in their inner circle?

Have gratitude and maintain a positive mental attitude.

CHAPTER 4

WORKJOCKEY WISDOM

It's easy to give advice and difficult to take it.

A WorkJockey doesn't just follow conventional wisdom. Focus instead on your goals and determine the most rapid and logical path for the attainment of your success. First define what success looks like for you. Most people have never really given this much thought; they are simply blowing in the wind. Be stronger than that. Set your course and don't let anyone or anything stand in your way or blow you off course.

Napoleon Hill described this as *definiteness of purpose.* I call it *obsessive pursuit of success. Obsessive* might seem too harsh a word; however, to simply try or wish is not enough. Remove internal roadblocks to success before concerning yourself with roadblocks that others place in your way. And you can be sure that there will be many roadblocks and distractions along the way. What distinguishes a winning athlete from any other? It is the relentless pursuit of the impossible or improbable. But everything was impossible in this world before someone made it possible.

In 1961 President John F. Kennedy told Congress that the United States should go to the moon in the next ten years, even though it seemed impossible. On July 20th, 1969, Neil Armstrong stepped onto the face of the moon. What seemed impossible in 1961 happened just eight years later. Anything is possible.

Wisdom comes not only from time and experience, it also comes from removing distractions and conclusions made by others. We have yet to determine the capacity of mankind. What is even more exciting is that we never will. How exciting the future will be for you and me and for those who follow after us.

There are three facets of wisdom to consider if you want to become a wise WorkJockey:

- Your current level of wisdom
- Your process for seeking wisdom
- Your future wisdom

Your current level of wisdom is influenced by all of your life and educational experiences, whether good or bad. No matter what your life has been like, you can improve your present and your future. You can do nothing to change your past. Your past is no longer important except as a reference.

Taking charge of you and everything you do is critical. Many have influenced your life and many more will influence your future. Control your affiliations with others and surround yourself with the kinds of people who inspire and influence you to gain wisdom. Remove all influences from people and circumstances that will not help you arrive at your destinations. I used the plural "destinations" on purpose. Life and success are about many destinations, not any one destination alone.

If someone asked you if you are a success, and you said, "I was a success once," it wouldn't mean much. Success is not an event, and neither is failure, according to my mentor, Zig Ziglar. Success is a culmination of progress toward reaching your goals and destinations in life. It's about leading and living your life on your terms and not the terms of others. Failure is merely a learning opportunity. Only those who have failed can set themselves up for success.

A wise WorkJockey is

- Comfortable with a contrarian's viewpoint
- Defines success *for them*
- Obsessively pursues their success
- Understands that their history can influence their future
- Knows that their history does not dictate their future

Your process for seeking wisdom is important because where and how you obtain knowledge can help or hinder you. Never stop learning, and never stop taking action. Knowledge without action is useless, and action without learning and knowledge is insanity. Are you doing the same things you have always done? Some of those things have helped you along your path; others are simply bad habits. But don't reside in the past. Filter through what works and what will not work for your future. If you have valuable traits and morals that you believe help you, by all means keep them. I'm talking about changing habits that you know deep down interfere with your success or hinder your growth as a good human being.

Charlie "Tremendous" Jones said, "You are going to be the same person in five years as you are today, except for the people you meet and the books you read." Be an avid reader, and value your time with other people. They can teach you things that books and other documents never can, and rapidly. Study, locate places of knowledge, and find those with knowledge whom you trust and who will ultimately propel you forward.

It doesn't matter whether you get information online, from books, or directly from individuals; they are all important resources.

Your conscience will be your guide if you follow it. Napoleon Hill describes your conscience as your *judge advocate* – an internal source you can ask whether your opinions and decisions are right or wrong. Your conscience knows the answer. We sometimes ignore our conscience and move in the wrong direction, and with every action there are reactions and consequences. Good actions are generally followed by good reactions and good consequences, and bad actions are generally followed by bad reactions and bad consequences. Find as many sources for answers to your questions and challenges as you can, and sort through them until you find the ones you can commit to.

Actions have good or bad outcomes for you personally; however, actions that hurt others while you benefit have a price you will have to pay in the future. We all do what we believe works for us and our objectives. Sometimes doing what works for us results in others being hurt, but because we benefitted, we discount, dismiss, defend, or even rationalize the injury caused to others as long as we get what we want. You can simply look at Washington, D.C., to get a bird's-eye view of this mindset. Incentives and rewards must be aligned with the right behavior. Bad behavior must not be rewarded, either directly or indirectly. Economist Thomas Freidman said, and I paraphrase: If you wish to eliminate the corruption in Washington, D.C., you must first change the current incentives that reward corruption.

Your future wisdom is based on your mindset, your belief in doing what is right, and the establishment of habits and behaviors that manifest the results you seek. This may seem like an overwhelming mandate, but it's simpler than you think. After all, if you're still searching, you recognize that you don't have all the answers. But there's no need to reinvent the wheel. Begin from where you are now and consider what others have learned from where they have already been.

Yes, you might need to blaze a new trail; however, knowing how others received benefits can provide direction. For example, using a compass to find your way regardless of where the trail leads is still important. There are tools that identify shortcuts to your destinations. Be sure, though, that the tools are right for the job and the shortcuts are right for you.

Recently I met a young woman named Jordan who works as a waitress at Smitty's Barbeque. She is working her way through school and intends to be a nurse. She is very smart and personable, knows what she wants to accomplish, and is pursuing her goals. My friend Lance Stanley and I eat at Smitty's Barbeque quite often, and we ask to sit in her section. One day Lance encouraged me to talk to Jordan about her future and to recommend Dale Carnegie's CD set called *How to Win Friends and Influence People*. I decided to tell her why the audio was important to me and why I felt it might also help her. She appeared very interested. I agreed to lend it to her for a month so she could listen to it and decide whether it was worth purchasing for herself.

Keep in mind I was not selling audios, I was just exposing her to the author and his message, which has helped me in the past and continues to help me to this day. I asked that she return the CDs after she was finished listening to them, but no later than a month from then. She agreed to do this. Less than a month later Lance and I were back in the restaurant and Jordan said she had listened to some of the CDs but wanted to return them now because she did not feel she would listen to them all before the month was up.

I discussed this with Lance and we determined that just because I had been ready to receive Carnegie's messages didn't mean she was. There is a saying, *When the student is ready, the teacher will appear.* I believe this is true for everyone, and it appeared she was not ready at her age or maybe at her maturity level in life.

This is not the first time I have tried to provide a helpful message to a younger person. Nearly a year earlier Lance and I met another young waitress named Hannah. I offered her the use of a different audio entitled *The Science of Personal Achievement* by Napoleon Hill. She assured us that she would listen to it right away and then return it. The next time we returned, she was no longer employed there. At the time of this writing Hannah had not returned the audio.

I learned a valuable lesson from these two events. Not everyone is ready to learn or to be inspired by a message or messenger. When you become enlightened, discover a great movie, or lose weight, you tend to think it's time that everyone follow in your footsteps. But if you think back, you'll remember how long it took you to prepare yourself to begin a new journey. I like this saying: Everything in good time. And the good time for you might not be the good time for someone else. Your successful future depends on your future wisdom.

Objective advice comes from the removal of emotion and the logic and maturity of wisdom.

CHAPTER 5

BREAK BAD HABITS BEFORE THEY BREAK YOU!

Are you sitting around waiting to die or waiting to live? Either way you are waiting. Dying will take care of itself. The living is all up to you. Life does not find you – you must find life.

Our lives are made up of a series of habits that we create over time. Do you believe you intentionally adopt behavior that places you in harm's way? Harm can come in the form of decreasing health or self-defeating personality traits. I am referring to persistent habits that develop into harmful behavior.

A Wake-Up Call

In 2012 I attended the HR [Human Resources] Florida State Conference in Orlando, Florida. They had a health screening booth in the expo hall, and I decided I would pop over and get a quick cardiovascular screening. I was there mainly because it was what everyone was doing, and did not expect what happened next. Two young women connected me to cuffs on both arms and took my blood pressure. Another woman checked my arteries and the flow of blood. When they were finished they said they had good news and bad news. I always like to hear the bad news first, so they told me I needed to see a physician soon. "Your blood pressure is off the charts." I asked, "So what is the good news?" They said, "You have great arteries and terrific blood flow." I knew I was obese, but I had preferred to live on a river in Egypt (denial). I weighed 250, at 5'9", with a 42" stretch waist; at least I had purchased 42" stretch pants – in short I had a 44" waist. I had high blood pressure and had been prescribed cholesterol medicine.

We are all good at giving advice and rarely good at taking it. I had written an article in 2007 about two things you must do if you are overweight. Neither were Nutrisystem or Weight Watchers. (Not that these programs don't help you lose weight; they do.) The bottom line of the article was that you must eat less and exercise more (provided you don't have a medical condition that prohibits exercise). Now it was time to follow my own advice. I embarked on a program of weight loss and fitness and found the real me underneath it all.

As the saying goes, there's an app for that. I used Runkeeper and Loseit! to track exercise and calories. I started July 7th, 2012, and by July 12th, 2014, I had lost eight-seven pounds and weighed 165. I have leveled to a comfortable weight of 175 and work to maintain this. I am off all medications, my blood pressure is normal, and my resting pulse is less than forty-five. My friend Lance recently adopted the same regimen and has dropped eighty pounds. For the first time in his life he is off insulin for type 2 diabetes. With focus and perseverance, you, too, can make uncomfortable but productive changes in your life. First inventory, then evaluate, and finally take action.

Elements in our society actually foster overeating and becoming obese. We are enabled to be rude and insulting, to take drugs, and to do other things our parents wouldn't be proud of. Did your school lunchroom promote eating everything on your plate so you could receive more? Do spouses sometimes make everything okay for the alcoholic in the family, the drug addict, or the domestic abuser? If they make everything functional for the dysfunctional, why in the world would their partner change their behavior? Why would a tattletale employee or a bad leader change their behavior when we continue to reward them with increased pay, promotions, new jobs, and new opportunities? We are all guilty at one time or another of promoting, supporting, or enabling bad behavior.

Is the personal pain of changing worth the gain? This is the most important question. No one will tell you that losing a few pounds is a bad idea. No one will tell you that you shouldn't do unto others as you would like them to do unto you. But there is a tipping point that you reach where the need to change weighs heavily enough that you decide to endure a little pain for the greater gain of changing harmful behavior. And you have to make a clear choice internally before you can change your external behavior.

Too Busy to Change?

After speaking with employees, managers, supervisors, and CEOs, I have found that unsuccessful people have one thing in common: they are "too busy" to get things done. I talk with them about the need to reduce and manage paperwork and create a paperless system in their workplace; they say they haven't the time. Either I didn't sell the benefits of saving time, or they just didn't get it. The Pareto principle states that 80 percent of the things we do don't accomplish a thing, while

20 percent of the things we do make all the difference in the world. This principle challenges the theory that we are too busy to improve performance, revealing that freeing up even a little more time allows us to do more important things like improving performance.

Are you too busy living to create a meaningful life?

Are you too busy working to create a meaningful career?

Are you too busy managing to become an organizational leader?

Are you too busy because being busy is the only thing you know how to do?

Did you know that Warren Buffet only works three hours a day? Obviously someone with his wealth doesn't have to work at all. How do you think people like him get that way? I assure you they don't get that way by being too busy to create the life they desire. They set aside time to plan and balance their lives beyond showing up day after day performing the same tasks and maintaining the status quo. They make plans and aren't afraid to change to achieve their goals.

Stephen Covey once proclaimed you should "Begin with the end in mind." I have spoken with supervisors, managers, and CEOs who say they are too busy to do another thing or to do something new or different. Take a breath and hold on, because you must stop telling yourself you are too busy. You are not too busy to get exactly what you want out of life, your job, and your relationships.

It just takes making informed choices. "Doing the same thing over and over again and expecting different results" is how Albert Einstein described insanity. Do you think Albert, as the inventor of many things, knew a thing or two about this concept? After all, if he had done the same thing over and over he wouldn't be in the history books today. Make time to do things differently today or you'll be in exactly the same circumstances or worse tomorrow. I'm not really telling you anything you don't already know, but perhaps you have not reached your tipping point and have not recognized or visualized your next steps or the need to change.

It's never too late to decide to make changes. We have all heard of the five Ps: Proper Planning Prevents Poor Performance. No truer statement has ever been uttered. Do you feel the need to follow those who have gone before you? Why are you so afraid to blaze a new trail? I know it's easy to avoid changing paths, and you are too busy – I get it. I'm not suggesting you reinvent every wheel, but I do suggest you challenge today's process if you plan to improve your future.

The buck begins and ends with you. Decisions must be made individually before they can be made organizationally. So don't get so busy conducting your day-to-day business that you cannot see the holes in the road ahead. You will never again be where you are today. You will never be younger or more in control. Don't let each and every moment pass you by without your involvement. When you think you are too busy, remember the 80/20 principle and think again!

Are you living your dream... or just chasing chickens?

What is it that causes an alcoholic, drug abuser, or domestic abuser to change? They may change when they discover the real hurt they are causing themselves and others. But change can only occur if they recognize the situation, make a choice, and become determined to persistently practice new, healthier behaviors.

Changing most unwanted behavior requires approximately twenty-one consecutive days of implementation. But for the addicted it can be a lifetime vigil. No matter what the behavior, a habit can be changed when the pain of not changing it becomes greater than the pain of change.

Studies have indicated that behavior and learning go hand and hand. For behavior to change, learning must occur. For example, a puppy goes to the bathroom in the house. You immediately place his nose within smelling range of the deed. Then you put the puppy outside. You do this each and every time it happens without fail. You know your message has been received the first time he lets you know he wants to go outside to do his business in the yard. The puppy soon learns not to repeat the bad behavior. When he returns to the house you reinforce the new behavior with warm praise, petting, and maybe even a doggie treat.

Think for a moment about a more immediate result from a stimulus: when you touched a hot object and snatched your hand away. The learning was immediate. It didn't require a learning curve. You just did not do that again.

Friends, co-workers, and acquaintances should not accept bad behavior from you. Don't provide excuses and try to justify behavior that is toxic and harmful to others. If you are unable to see your behavior for what it is, others, especially those who care about you, will have to point it out and help you change. They require a change if you are to remain in their employment or relationship. We should not enable others to continue behaving badly if they are doing harm.

We all have bad habits, and I'm certainly no exception to that rule. In elementary school I was taught to overeat. The school system believed it was promoting healthy behavior by telling students to eat everything on their plates so they could have more and/or a favorite dessert. Children, and adults for that matter, should learn to eat only when they are hungry. Today I still struggle with leaving food on my plate. I have broken the habit of eating everything, but I still feel guilty about leaving food on my plate.

As informed adults we have a choice to change our behavior. Most who deal with a weight problem realize that it's not a diet they need, but a lifestyle change. Like many of you who are reading this, I have lost hundreds of pounds, one at a time, with one miracle diet after another. But the cold hard fact is that it's a two-part formula: exercise more and eat less. This lifestyle adjustment guarantees success every time, unless you have a medical problem that interferes.

Any behavior that puts you or someone else at risk of injury or illness is bad behavior. Have you ever rolled through a stop sign? You might have done this consciously the first time, and it was okay as long as no car was coming. Perhaps it then became standard practice. At first a conscious choice was made to overlook the rule, but then the sign was ignored altogether and the subconscious driver in you took over, creating a habit of rolling through without stopping and looking both ways. You found yourself unintentionally rolling through stop signs without looking because you trained your body this way.

When my family moved to a new neighborhood, I drove to the old house after work two days in a row! Obviously this habit cost me only time. But other habits can cost a great deal more.

Make a conscious choice to carefully make the right choices day by day, celebrating each success when breaking bad habits, and soon you will be healthier, happier, and on your way to controlling your destiny. There are no quick fixes. Develop a plan to change behavior that might be slowly yet definitely destroying you. As soon as you decide the pain is worth the gain, get started!

Addictive behavior can make the task of changing more difficult. Relapses are likely to occur. Relapses are not failures unless and until you accept them as failures. Determining which behavior needs to change is only a small part. You have to plan and maybe even seek outside help to change, but you can do it! Many people have overcome far greater circumstances with far fewer resources than are available today. And when you are successful you will manifest the strength, courage, and knowledge to help others. Start today by breaking bad habits before they break you.

I don't regret my past... because it has taught me how to live for the future.

CHAPTER 6

WHEN THE GOING GETS TOUGH

I can show you the path of least resistance OR the path of greatest results.

You might have already begun to apply the principles of becoming a WorkJockey. As you master these concepts you will earn the title WorkJockey. We are beginning this chapter with the principles for creating habits that will help you when times are tough and it's easier to drift back into old habits. Being a lifelong WorkJockey requires a commitment to set aside many of your thought processes. You will continue your study and growth as someone who realizes that there is much more to life than work.

As mentioned previously, work is a tool, just like a hammer or a wrench. It allows us to survive and thrive and is a necessary part of our lives. Make the most of work; it should not be about how many hours you work. Work is about results and not about time. You are becoming a WorkJockey because this makes sense to you. You have been mentally challenged to follow the mantras of the past: work longer and harder so reward will find you. But you are not going to wait for the future for your reward. You will not be one of those who work until retirement only to die shortly thereafter, not having lived.

Many of my supervisors died shortly after retirement, and some even died prior to retirement. All the money in the world is not worth that. Keep in mind that most folks who work long and hard rarely maintain a significant portion of their income into retirement. Many are dependent on social security income that may or may not be available. Even if social security is still around when you retire, it will not be enough to live comfortably, nor was it intended to be.

Make a plan long before you retire to save and establish more than one stream of income. If you can do this you can maintain your membership as a WorkJockey. If you cannot create a successful strategy you will be forced to work long and hard into what some call the golden years.

If you have read this far and have begun to change your focus and take action, you are a WorkJockey. This journey is different for each person, beginning at different ages and with different backgrounds and mindsets. Recall the saying *When the student is ready the teacher will appear.* I hope you are ready and I hope others who read this book or hear this message are ready. If not, I can only hope they will pick up this book later when they are ready to make some changes.

Life is fragile for everyone. Even those with a strategy and a plan don't know how long they have. Don't put off living for the sake of life. Make a difference by swimming upstream and follow the WorkJockey principles to get where you want to go. Track your membership in the WorkJockey clan. All roads do not lead to this membership. There will be detours, obstacles, and people who will challenge you to stop.

After reading this book you should have the strength and will power to make the necessary changes in your life. You will be in the minority. The majority will try to stop you. Some will try to stop you directly, intentionally; and others will try because they think you will fail and they want to protect you from failure. They are not protecting you, and their good intentions won't mean anything to you in the end. Down deep you must be strong. Your gut instinct has already kicked in and provides the strength to fight off the naysayers.

Refer back to *WorkJockey* and its principles often. It should be like exercise: you can't stop, otherwise you will become weak and unable to defend against attack. I'm not trying to scare you; I'm trying to prepare you for what will come between you and your success. Just ask any celebrity, performer, athlete, or entrepreneur. They recall the manmade obstacles they faced while clawing their way to success. Many did not make it. A few were able to thrive. No matter what, they all had to pay some dues along the way.

It's easy to give up just before you reach critical success. Once you have a true taste of the WorkJockey lifestyle, no one can take it away or convince you to slow down or stop. You have the formula to keep on keeping on.

You are a WorkJockey now. What does that mean to you? What does your lifestyle look like now that you have changed your thinking and your behavior? Whenever you need a dose of reality, think what you would do differently if you were rich. What work would you do if money were no object? With that in mind, consider your financial needs and work backwards. For example, if you need $50K per year to support your lifestyle, find a way to earn that much through your current employment or by providing a value-based product or service that will generate this income. Let the amount of income you need guide your thinking. Include paying your bills, feeding your family, and any other needs that must be met. Resist the urge to spend more time on work; consider how to be more productive in less time at work.

Over time your strength will improve and no one will be able to interfere with your successful transformation. Think about a bodybuilder's determination to get down to 4 to 6 percent body fat to compete on stage. I have never had that kind of desire or dedication. They truly put their minds to it, and many do not have a spouse doing the same thing for support and encouragement. They go to restaurants with their friends and don't partake of the food and drink to excess. That is true control and dedication to a goal. Even when I lost eighty-seven pounds, it took twenty-four months of work, but that was only the beginning. To lose weight is one thing, but to keep it off takes even more stamina in maintaining your new lifestyle.

My friend Lance decided to get one up on me. He lost eighty pounds in only eighteen months. Wow, he nailed it hard. We both tracked our calories and yet he put even more cardio work in and made his mind up about how hard he was willing to work. He told me that the straw that broke the camel's back was when I offered him my fat clothes that I had grown out of.

Now you have the courage to continue if you have read and applied what you have learned up to this point. This is where maintenance is a factor. Begin with the idea that you will only work forty hours a week (even if you are salaried). If circumstances or situations require otherwise, you can be sure you are running off track with your strategy. I can hear you now: "But I have to work more than that, at least sometimes." I understand your predicament, but establish a forty-hour baseline and work from that point.

If you cannot negotiate a forty-hour work week at this time, work on performance and efficiencies so that in the future you can negotiate from a position of strength. Salaried employees especially are up against old management styles and mindsets. You cannot be a slug or lazy and expect any consideration or be able to negotiate in the future. Only high-performing employees have this flexibility. The slug will be forced to improve performance or be removed.

Flexibility has penetrated the work force. Employers are learning that to keep the best and brightest they must meet employees' needs. This is a new formula for the engaged work force. Employees who ask, "What's in it for me?" are no longer taboo. You hear a lot about millennials, generation Xers, and Boomers. I challenge the conventional wisdom that what employees want is based on their date of birth. First, most folks don't have a full understanding of what it is they want. And if they do, it changes from year to year, and employers have to reevaluate rewards and incentives in order to keep up. Organizations try to clone you once they understand that less is actually more. Less time equals more productivity.

There are other benefits of flexibility for the employer that will be realized as well: reduced absenteeism, reduced turnover, fewer worker's compensation claims, higher levels of customer service, and better overall customer experiences. There are many other positive results that come from working less, living more, accomplishing more, and being happier. There is a learning curve for employees and employers. Once on the other side of the learning curve, your behavior will be the norm and others will be adopting this new behavior to keep up. There will always be the slugs, the lazy employees, and the opportunists. They stand out like the proverbial sore thumbs. But they will only survive in broken organizations that haven't figured this out.

I predict that in the next decade human potential will accelerate along with technology. Some people and organizations will be left behind, but you will not be one of them. You will be able to write your own ticket. You will have opportunities that did not exist earlier in your career. You might be self-employed, or working with an organization on your terms. Keep on keeping on, and even take others along who are willing to travel with you. The journey to your success is no fun by yourself, and no one is self-made in the end. Enjoy the journey, and take someone with you.

CHAPTER 7

WORKING WISELY

Don't just focus or take action...
take focused action.

Cycle of Silliness

When I was a police officer I saw detectives, officers, sergeants, and others working off-duty and overtime to maximize income to support their toys – toys like jet skis, boats, motorcycles, etc. that their regular paycheck could not have paid for. The problem, as you might imagine, was that the income from these extracurricular activities was not permanent. When officers received promotions that resulted in less overtime and subsequently less income, they would find themselves in bankruptcy court and even in divorce court. We are sometimes our own worst enemy, and our organizations are the enablers.

I confess that at one time I got caught up in this behavior too. It cost me my marriage. Of course it wasn't the sole reason for the divorce, but it was a contributing factor. George Strait sang, "I never saw a hearse with a luggage rack." Those words make sense. You can't take it with you. You will never get out alive. Based on interview after interview of people on their deathbed, none of them proclaimed, "I wish I had worked more hours." However, nearly all of them might have wished they had *worked less, lived more, and been happier.*

Let's examine the all-too-often-mentioned forty-hour work week. It has been the staple of full-time employment for a very long time now – so long that we've almost forgotten where it came from. Rumor has it that Ford Motor Company originated the forty-hour week.

The forty-hour week is not really the problem as I see it. The problem is we have continued to exceed the forty-hour week with overtime, part-time assignments, off-duty work, and working after work. We work too much and produce too little. Study after study revealed that when participants worked longer hours, productivity decreased and in some cases became nonexistent. Yes, we are on the clock longer, but we are compensated for less and less productivity. Whether we work overtime on the job or at work somewhere else, it hurts productivity and damages health and family relationships.

Employers should pay particular attention because I'm going to focus on the word *engagement* for a moment. Many articles and books are written every day about employee engagement. You cannot garner employee engagement when your employees are tired, distracted, and burned out. All the motivation in the world cannot help until you address this element first. Employees must work less to perform more. This is contrary to what most of us have been taught. More hours, more time on the job, does not generally produce or create better results. Short periods of additional workload are not the problem; the culture that exists today in which more work supposedly produces more results is the problem. It does not help the organization or employees to continually overwork employees.

Salaries are another form of abuse in some organizations. Salaries have been helpful for employers in budgeting payroll. Rather than calculating hours, organizations budget more directly based on fixed salaries. But depending on the industry, other abuses began to occur. Particularly in the retail industry, some stores work employees excessively under the salary umbrella. It may be legal to a point, but the end result is the same. In organizations that are less ethical, it amounts to abuse. The ability to designate an employee as a salaried employee does not apply to all employees. The Equal Employment Opportunity Commission (EEOC) has a list of employee categories considered appropriate for a salary. I am not opposed to salaries as long as the employee also benefits from the arrangement and is treated fairly.

Whether or not it is legal does not change the premise. If you are salaried and working extensive hours beyond the traditional forty per week, it should be the exception, not the rule. The EEOC is always looking to provide additional regulations to mitigate inequities; however, their focus is on proper compensation rather than proper work periods.

No amount of money is worth losing your health, your family, or your future. To maintain WorkJockey status, fight off the temptation to work more, and fend off the unethical employer who insists you prove your loyalty by working for endless, unlimited periods of time.

Ask yourself, "Which is more valuable, my time or my talent and training?" Your talent and training can be increased; your time cannot. Therefore your time, *not* your talent or training, is most valuable to you. If your supervisors made a shift, too, they would know this as well and the situation could become a win-win for everyone.

Talent and training can improve performance, create solutions, improve outcomes, and get to the goal line faster than simply throwing more work hours at a challenge. A friend of mine named Martin Ferrell told me an interesting story: A man came into a television repair shop begging the owner to fix his television in a hurry so he could watch the Super Bowl. The repairman said he could fix it for $200. The customer agreed. The repairman had his son remove the back of the television and replace a bulb, and the set was fixed in only a few minutes. The customer became irate and did not want to pay $200 for a new bulb that a kid could replace. The owner of the shop said, "You are not paying me for the time or the blub, you are paying me for the technical knowledge I have gained over time that enabled me to tell my son how to fix your television. If you had that knowledge, you wouldn't have come in here today asking me for help."

Your talent is very important to your success and the success of your employer. You should be hired for your talent. However, you only have a set amount of time in which to use that talent to build yourself a great life. Just because your employer wants you to work a lot of overtime or put you on a salary, you don't have to agree if it will harm your plans to create a good life for yourself and your family.

Think differently and learn to value your time as your most important and valuable asset. Guard it from those who would take advantage of your time to get all of your talent. Remember this the next time you apply for a promotion or a new job.

Tips to remember:

- WorkJockeys think differently.
- Work less to accomplish more.
- Your time is most important to you.
- Your talent is most important to your employer.

What does your employer want from you? What do you and other employees want from your employer? These two questions make up what I call the *employee/employer bridge*. Both employees and employers have desires that are not mutually exclusive. Both can get what they want. You might be thinking that one has to triumph over the other. This is far from the truth. Only when an employee understands what their employer wants, and gives it to them, can they in turn expect to get what they want as well. This is the mindset of a WorkJockey. When you understand what your employer really wants, you can decide whether or not you can provide it. You are in control of that decision, no one else.

To get ahead in your job, or find a better one, a WorkJockey needs keen insight into what's really happening at work. Very basically, the organization you work for was founded for a purpose. It matters not whether it's a non-profit, governmental, or for-profit venture; it was founded on the premise of filling a need or a desire in the marketplace. To master the bridge you must have a good grasp of the "why" in your organization. Why does the organization exist? Why have you been hired? What are you expected to do in your role for the organization to meet its needs so it can in turn meet the needs of its customers and employees?

It's important to learn this before you can accurately plan how to best serve your organization. I write much about serving and service in this book. If you are not providing a valuable service, your position and future opportunities may be in jeopardy.

We have all heard that employees are replaceable. This is very true if you work like a commodity, doing your work in a manner that is easy for others to replicate. But valued employees are not so easily replaced – attitudinally, behaviorally, or in terms of skills. This changes the dynamic a bit. A WorkJockey strives to become so valuable that they are irreplaceable.

Your employer, and most important your immediate supervisor, should know this and should be reminded from time to time how valuable you are. Your value lies more in your attitude and behavior than in your specific skills. It's much easier to replace skills than to replace a great work ethic. Skills can be taught, but you can't teach a great attitude and personality. A WorkJockey with a great attitude and productive workplace behavior is worth their weight in gold. Employers don't mind losing problem employees but they prefer to keep their best and brightest.

Three areas to consider as a WorkJockey in regard to work:

- What's in for me (WIIFM)?
- What's in for them (WIIFT)?
- Why are we here; what is our purpose?

If you can successfully answer these questions, you are likely positioning yourself for higher earning and greater opportunities.

What's In It for Me?

Before you can adequately answer that question, first answer this one: "What do I want from my association with my organization?" I hope money is not your only objective. We all want to make all the money we can, but there is a balance to be reached between personal development, self-expression, and the financial achievement you seek. If it is all about money, your search for a lucrative position will be focused and strategic, and you will filter out opportunities without this component or so-called non-negotiable. If money, *opportunity, and service* fit into your goals, and I hope they do, you can broaden your filter.

You might have to satisfy a financial need in the immediate short term, settling for less than your true goals or intentions. Settling for money alone should be a temporary situation or you will never be truly happy in your life, particularly in your work life. Many settle for an entire lifetime, wishing all along the way that they had been a little more adventurous and willing to take calculated risks to pursue their goals. But you're a WorkJockey, so you will look beyond such a situation once you are back on your feet.

Move when the time is right, and don't wait until there is no time left or you will be sorry. Don't leave an opportunity until another one is available. My dad once told me, "Don't quit a job until you have another job to go to." Only once have I ever quit a job without having another one lined up, and I got busy finding another job right away.

Consider other things you might want from your employment. What about having interesting work? What about working in a great culture? What about being able to have a flexible schedule that allows you time to do more outside of work? Can you work fewer hours per day or fewer days per week than the norm to get that extra time? Some employers are now willing to negotiate such things, and more are becoming willing. Be clear in your mind about your ideal employment opportunity so you can determine which items on your master list of requirements you can compromise on. If you are a WorkJockey with a strong personal brand and a smart skillset, you can negotiate from strength when you know what your employer or perspective employer wants. When you are just starting out you might need to take the best opportunity you can find even if it's not perfect. A WorkJockey knows that jobs are not forever, and you can move from one position to a better one in time.

What's In It for Them?

The employer wishes to meet a need, satisfy the mandates of their management, and serve their customer base. They need satisfied customers, happy customers, and most important, repeat customers. They must keep risk at a minimum, loss low, and opportunities high. They need to know what their competition is doing and why they are doing it. Failure to see what's coming can result in lost organizational opportunities or even losing the entire organization in the marketplace.

Employers want high performance even though most are not sure what that means. Most want employees to do more with less. We have all heard those words uttered. (The truth is that we should have been trying to do more with less before financial crisis was upon us.) They want the biggest bang for their payroll buck. Employers with high turnover are reluctant to invest in thoroughly training an employee for fear the employee will leave and take that training and knowledge with them. They should know, as famous motivational speaker Zig Ziglar once said, "The only thing worse than training an employee and having them leave, is to not train them and have them stay."

Many employers opened their business based solely on their expertise and not their ability to manage the business. This places them at great risk. They have a product or service in demand; however, the task of managing the operational aspects of the business is foreign to them. Great examples are doctors and lawyers. They are professionally trained to deliver a service, yet they are the de facto leaders and owners of their businesses and are expected to have business management skills sufficient to manage their practices. Many survive due primarily to the small scope of such a professional practice. Not all of them remain small, and growth multiplies their management challenges exponentially. They can use some help, but they have to be willing to let someone help with management so they can do what they do best – stand and deliver their services.

Why Are We Here; What Is Our Purpose?

Owners and administrators generally know the answer to this question. Rank and file staff may have an overall idea yet not fully appreciate the true dynamics involved. Who else can or does offer your product or service? Is your product or service better than the competition's? If so, how is it better? If not, what about the competition should you be worried about?

There are a lot of questions without a whole lot of answers here. If your product or service is treated like a commodity, you will struggle beyond price. Growth will be an issue, and many variables beyond your control can result in defeat. I have owned four businesses – two that made money and two that did not. So I have been on both sides of the equation. One of those businesses was a package and mail service called The Mail Room. Shortly after I purchased the business, there were two major mergers in the industry. United Parcel Service (UPS) bought the Mailbox Etcetera franchise, and then Federal Express (FedEx) bought the Kinko's franchise. These mergers made my business impossible to maintain. All I could do was follow my attorney's advice, lock the doors, walk away, and declare bankruptcy. This was quite a financial shock to me, and far beyond my control. In today's climate a business must always be trying to improve far beyond its current capabilities.

It is important to remember that organizational purpose and objectives change over time. The intent of the organization when it was founded can be very different from what it evolved into, and the needs of customers might have changed. A pay phone company likely lost that business long ago unless they found a niche market: parks, public institutions, etc. Smart WorkJockeys pay attention to the marketplace and evaluate whether the purpose of their current employer is still relevant.

Whether you are seeking promotion or want to change employers, remember that the employer makes the hiring decision. What they do *not* do is determine your value. You must create and market your value. Employers see your opportunity as simply another filled position. They eventually see you as indispensable and valuable beyond your compensation. But you don't want to be seen as fulfilling only a specific role or job function because you might become unpromotable, and this will interfere with your growth and other opportunities.

Remember:

- Your goals and your employer's goals are not mutually exclusive.
- Mind your attitude, behavior, and skills.

- Pay attention to the purpose of your organization and whether it's still relevant.
- Seek to become indispensable to your employer. You control when you want to make a change instead of being at the mercy of your supervisor.

Any organization that is not changing is dying a slow death.

CHAPTER 8

AIM FOR HIGH PERFORMANCE

I've never had a job that wasn't a great job. If you put your attitude in the right place – my dad taught me this – every job is a good job. I used to dig ditches and wax floors for Tom P. Haney Vocational Technical Center in Panama City, Florida. My supervisor there, Mr. Ed Bond, gave me a terrific recommendation that opened the doors to my career in law enforcement. I treated that job with enthusiasm and a high-performance mindset. That attitude created great results, so I carried it with me to every job I ever worked.

Having a high-performance mindset means you analyze everything you do to determine what value your labor produces for you and your organization. A WorkJockey pays attention at work and finds ways to improve their performance and the performance of the organization. That routine that everyone does that wastes time and energy – how about figuring out a better way?

I met a man who was an expert in recycling. He told me the best way to get people to recycle is to make sure the recycling bins are easier to get to than the trash cans. All he did was reposition the trash cans and recycling bins in offices and factories, and companies saved money and helped the environment. Sometimes being a high performer means making a simple, common-sense change to something that's otherwise taken for granted.

A high-performing WorkJockey has an open mind and is always looking for ways to save time, money, or effort for their employer. Ask yourself questions like these:

- How can I make this easier?
- Where do we waste time?
- What tasks or procedures are real pains in the neck? Is there a way to fix or eliminate them?
- What do customers complain about? Can I find a solution?

WorkJockeys know that they can contribute great ideas at work even if they are not members of a management team. The people who do the work often have insights that desk-bound leaders can't imagine. When you contribute ideas to improve your work, others notice and begin to respect your thinking.

WorkJockeys also realize that mistakes happen on the job in spite of best intentions. It does not pay to spend a lot of time blaming yourself or others when a mistake occurs. Instead, accept responsibility if you made the error, and focus on finding a solution.

I can show the path of least resistance or the path to the greatest results.

To reach high performance you must go from A = Average to B = Best. Think of it like an old Swiss watch. If there's a glitch in that watch, it's not going to work. For example, if there are ten employees and if they're really going to pursue high performance, all ten have to be firing on all cylinders. And they're not going to do that based on a policy manual or because it's dictated. They're going to do it because they choose to... almost like they're working for a volunteer organization except that they draw paychecks. The idea is to treat people with dignity and respect and value their work.

What every leader and manager wants is the highest level of performance from their employees, and employees find it exciting to work for a high-performance company. They feel secure. They know their paychecks are not going to bounce. They feel the organization is going somewhere and they want to go with it; that they have a future there.

There are benefits to fully showing up for work and making a contribution so that working together is exciting and you're constantly moving forward. High performance is like crime prevention. Nobody thinks we should eliminate law enforcement simply because we'll never wipe out all crime; that would be ridiculous. It's the same with high performance; you never fully arrive, but you pursue it. And that improves you and the entire organization and its staff.

You never fully arrive at highest performance because we're all human. We're not computers. We have life struggles like bankruptcy and divorce. Someone might have taken a dive in their life and can only occasionally come up for air. Organizations have budget problems and separation issues, too. There is always some issue to deal with somewhere.

But relationships between employees, and between employees and managers, should be as close as they possibly can. A marriage cannot survive unless both partners are in love.

An employee and employer are married in a way, or at least you could refer to them as partners in the organization. They must work together in harmony in order to achieve success.

It comes down to every employee giving their best. The highest level of performance would be for every employee to give all they've got, all the time. Now that's not reality, and it's never going to be reality. But as in the crime-prevention analogy, that's what everyone should pursue.

You might be wondering why you should care about giving your best at your job, especially if you don't like your work. A WorkJockey knows that striving to do your best is always worth it. If you don't like your job, do your very best for that employer so you can learn and work your way into a better position. Little hinges swing big doors. Your job today can provide the stepping stone to a better one tomorrow. A high-performing WorkJockey is a valuable asset to any organization because of their ability to find ways to be more efficient and productive. Doing your best at work is always worthwhile.

CHAPTER 9

WORKJOCKEY COMMUNICATION TIPS

I used to teach interviewing and interrogation, and I use those skills to this day. Will being able to read people effectively help you in your everyday employment? The answer is yes, especially when it comes to people's facial expressions as opposed to what they say verbally.

A WorkJockey realizes the value of communication, including being able to assess people and situations, and picking up on subtle clues.

Start with Listening

One of the easiest ways to excel at your work is to improve your listening skills. People today are distracted, often multitasking, and trying to have conversations while looking at their phones. Listening is an art that enhances any career.

To improve your listening skills, use these steps:

- Look the other person in the eye and pay attention. This is a sign of respect.
- Focus on the other person. Put down your phone or stop what you're doing. If you're not able to stop what you're

doing in that moment, ask if you can meet later so you can give the other person your full attention.

- Wait to speak until the other person is finished.
- Ask questions. If something is not clear or you need more detail, ask.
- Paraphrase what you heard back to the other person to ensure it is accurate. I learned this from interviewing suspects. If I did not ensure the accuracy of what I heard, an investigation could be compromised. It is important to ensure that you understand what the other person is saying.

To build trust, reduce conflict, and improve communication, it's better to over-communicate a bit than to not communicate thoroughly enough. Think of drinking from a fire hose. Provide your co-workers with as much information as you can until they say, "Whoa! I've got it." The reason I know this works is that it's saved my butt many times in making sure my supervisors knew what I was doing.

For example, my supervisor, Commander David Slusser, once called me to his office to chew me out. He was chewing me up one side and down the other. It was almost funny, because I was thinking, "What you're chewing me out about – I didn't do any of that." So finally I just said, "Sir, when you finish, I'll tell you the rest of the story. I'd be happy to tell you."

He said, "You tell me now!"

I said, "I told my supervisors every step of the way what I was doing, and they knew at all times what I was doing."

My supervisors were sitting right there. He looked at them and asked, "Is that true?"

They said yes.

He said, "You're excused."

These were all guys who liked me, including the commander. Nobody was ever against me. They liked me because I was always stepping up to the plate and I had a very good attitude. The commander never apologized. I'm sure he told himself, like most supervisors, "Oh well, he understands I just made a mistake." I did understand that, but he should have admitted that he had made a mistake.

The lesson here is to over-communicate for success, and invest as much time in an apology as you do in a reprimand. I learned a valuable lesson from this incident for my future success as a supervisor. The communication can't be one way. It has to travel in both directions. That's why I say it's not complicated, but it is hard work. And both people have to actively listen.

Clear Communication Requires Time

Communicating clearly is worthwhile for every WorkJockey. Yes, it's more time-consuming to communicate clearly and precisely. We're used to regurgitating information and asking, "You got it?" And everybody says yes because they're too embarrassed to say no. You walk away and nobody's got it, or they think they got it and yet it was misunderstood. We're always in too big of a hurry.

When I'm speaking in front of a group, I assume that about 10 percent of the people are going to get what I give them. We're so distracted at all times. I ask the group, "Wouldn't it be great if you didn't have to repeat yourself?" Everybody says yeah. Then I tell them, "Forget it. It's never going to happen."

Marketing professionals could save a lot of money if they only had to show an advertisement one time and everybody got it. But that has never happened in the history of the world. And it's never going to happen. You have to repeat the important things – to the point that they say, "I've got you, I'm with you, and I'm on board." Once they have validated what you're saying, you've actually completed your communication. It's not hard to do, but there's a lot of work involved.

Barriers to Communication

Your tone of voice and facial expression, and the other person's tone of voice and facial expression, can interfere with the communication process. Let's say you're doing really well and I want to convey that. I should prepare for that interview. I know that sounds weird, but what I mean is I shouldn't just walk into your office on the fly and say, "Hey, I just want to tell you you're doing a great job on that project." It means virtually nothing. I didn't tell you what it is you're doing that I approve of so you can give me more of that and less of what I don't like (which I didn't identify either).

I used to tell people I trained in interviewing suspects that you must mentally prepare for the interview because you have only one chance to make a first impression, and if you make the wrong impression the odds of coming out of there with the information you're after are slim. Don't try to wing it.

It is also important to communicate with enthusiasm. No one is inspired by someone who won't make eye contact and speaks in a dull, boring tone. If you want to lead or influence others – and good WorkJockeys do, learn to speak with enthusiasm and a sparkle in your eye. If you find speaking to others difficult, consider participating in Toastmasters or a Dale Carnegie course.

CHAPTER 10

WORKJOCKEYS AND WEALTH

Life is your oyster unless you bite into a pearl.

Being a WorkJockey requires that you place wealth and your financial status into perspective. It doesn't matter whether you're in debt, out of debt, or currently considered wealthy, because your financial situation can change in a moment. Instead of focusing on today's bank balance, determine a set of priorities and how you plan to finance them. Think of a luxury car versus a very nice car that meets your needs. It is all about perspective. I'm not telling you to avoid dreaming big; I'm saying don't place unreasonable expectations on yourself that make you feel envious and as though you are a victim of circumstance.

There are three areas of consideration I would like you to evaluate:

- Your wealth today
- Your wealth at your goal status
- Wealth in your future

Your Wealth Today

Let's begin with your wealth today. How much money do you have on hand? How much money do you make from your job or career? How much do you owe? This is a lot to think about, so take it one item at a time. If you are like most people, you're living paycheck to paycheck. If this is not your situation, congratulations, and you may move on to the next section.

If you're still with me, let's take a look at your fundamental finances. I will be honest and tell you I am not a big fan of budgets, though a budget might be where you need to start depending on your circumstances. Determine the balance point between your income and your debt. Once you clearly determine this tipping point, you can create a plan to get there. I like to think of this as a line item budget. This means something different to accountants and bookkeepers, but for this discussion it's very simple: Where does your money go every month, and how much, if any, is left over? If you don't have any left over, then you are balanced.

"Balanced" implies you are in good shape. But don't pat yourself on the back too quickly. This is a bad balance. You have no savings, no investments, and nothing for your future retirement (assuming you have not established a system for retirement income or included one in your balance calculations). It's time to take a good hard look at what you spend your money on. If you have never given this any thought, you might think there is no way you can save and certainly no way you can generate more income.

(Keep in mind that I'm talking about an individual's finances. If you have a family, that adds another layer to your planning process. Focus on your behavior before tackling family behavior.)

Itemize everything you spend money on. Determine the absolute necessities and how to save money on those necessities. If you are in serious debt, every other thing that does not meet the "necessity" category must be eliminated from your budget. I'm not saying that if you truly want or enjoy something you can't add it to your budget later; I'm saying at least a temporary sacrifice is necessary to establish a stable financial foundation.

Once you have eliminated luxuries and items you don't require to survive, reevaluate the balance. You will find you are out of balance, but this out-of-balance is a good thing for now, as you have created some extra money each month. This creates the opportunity to start saving for emergencies and retirement.

Your Wealth at Your Goal Status

Your wealth when you reach your financial goal is the next thing to tackle. What is your goal for wealth? How much do you want to make? This can change, of course, but for now we are talking about the immediate goals you have. For example, maybe you would like to be able to pay all your debts on time while saving some money for emergencies and a reasonable retirement. When you find you are doing this very well, it's time to revisit or recalculate your goals.

You might wish to add some luxuries, but wait. First determine what debts can be paid off completely. Obviously things like utilities, maintenance, property taxes, food, and clothing will never be paid off. There are other debts like cars, mortgages, etc. that can be eliminated, allowing you the luxury of increased retirement savings, travel, etc.

Wealth in Your Future

Now consider your goals for long-term wealth. Are you saving for retirement or to fund the things you really want? You might want to send your kids to college or be able to play golf every day after you stop working. (I used to play golf, but I could never get past the windmill on the course, so I quit playing.) These long-term goals are reachable if you start saving now.

Most of us are not financial experts. There is no shame in getting expert advice. I suggest consulting a good financial planner who can help you set up strategies to build the wealth you need for your future. The sooner you start, the easier it will be.

Providing wealth for your future requires jealously guarding your talent, resources, and time. You can, of course, get more talent, and you can get more resources, but you cannot get more time.

Take inventory of your current talents. What can you do? What can you do well? And most important, what do you want to do? This final question should help you tailor your future education and learning to remove roadblocks and other obstacles to pursuing what you like to do.

No one is good at everything; however, everyone is good at something. Focus on being specific about what you want to do and spend your time mastering the skills that allow you to do it. Attorneys, lawyers, doctors, and other professionals discover that specializing generally creates greater wealth and job and career satisfaction. Think about surgeons, bankruptcy attorneys, carpenters, singers, and many other professionals. The more they focus on specifics, the more success they generate, the easier it gets, and the more revenue they create. Everyone likes a specialist. You don't pay a doctor of psychiatry to take your tonsils out and you don't pay a chiropractor to operate on your vertebrae.

Things to consider:

- Fulfill your needs before your desires.
- Someone will always have *more* or *less* than you do.
- It is never about how much money you make; it's about how much you keep.
- If your finances are balanced, you are headed for trouble.
- Out-of-balance finances can be good *or* bad.
- Plan today for the future you want and start saving to create it.
- Guard your talent, resources, and time so that they contribute to your wealth today and tomorrow.

Doing a good job with a nasty attitude damages your assets.

CHAPTER 11

THE INNER GAME

Morals keep you ethical, ethics keep you legal,
and staying legal keeps you out of jail.

The most important thing to a WorkJockey is the kind of person you are and how you can continually develop into an even better person. Don't try to get what you want at the expense of others or by cheating your employer, clients, or others. Follow this premise: if it's moral, it's likely to be ethical; if it's ethical, it's likely to be legal; and if it's legal, let's face it – it will keep you out of jail.

The next most important element for a WorkJockey is understanding and prioritizing the motto *All work and no play….* Work must never become your life. Work is just a tool for realizing your dreams and goals. As mentioned above, Napoleon Hill espouses, "A goal is a dream with a deadline." A carpenter and a videographer have the tools of their trade. Tools are not items to hinder you but to assist you in whatever endeavor of employment you are engaged in. Your job is a tool you can use to create the future you want. This tool must be calibrated or even sharpened to help you achieve. True WorkJockeys don't let their work override their life. Work improves, enhances, and even prolongs life. Your job should not be about working until you die. Quality of work and life is key over quantity.

Make Memorable Moments

A WorkJockey has realized that life is not all about work; it's about creating a memorable life through memorable moments. If you are too busy working and making a living, you are unlikely to be creating those memorable moments and living a great life. Let's test this premise: If you received a large inheritance tomorrow, would you go on working? Many people say yes. However, when confronted with a few more days or weeks of work that provide no reward or financial incentive, they might quickly change perspective and ask the question "Why am I working here?" With no need for the income, they realize the work they're doing isn't all that much fun after all, and resign.

Study after study revealed that when folks were confronted with their mortality, they rarely wish they could have worked a little longer or worked more overtime. They realize, often too late, that working less and living more would have been a much better idea. By that time their health has suffered and possibly deteriorated to the point that their quality of life is jeopardized.

Learn to jockey your work to meet your needs while remaining important to your employer. Think of your personal time as having equal value as your work time. Only when you put your personal time into the equation will you make it part of your planning. Don't let it be an afterthought.

How can your time be better spent? Folks always tell me they are too busy. I believe them when they say this; however, rarely do they tell me they are truly productive by being busy. My experience tells me that much busy work is unproductive and a waste of time and resources.

Consider minimizing time and maximizing results. Though this might seem like an impossible task, it's not as difficult as you might think. But you do have to seek out opportunities to make it happen.

While I was consulting with a non-profit one time, a new legal dilemma presented itself. Wage and hour laws were being proposed that would require employers to revisit the overtime exemption equation for employees designated as exempt from overtime pay and eligible for a salary. The law would nearly double compensation for salaried employees. Your initial reaction might be, "This is great news for the employee." And yes, some employees would see an increase in their pay. But most would find either their pay or their hours reduced. A negative person would be upset about this. A positive person might see opportunity.

Let's look at the employer's side first. They are unlikely to increase all salaries to the higher, possibly double amount. Even if they wanted to, shouldering the expense of all the other factors involved such as matching social security and wage-based benefits would not make good business sense. This is why I believe they would reduce or in some cases eliminate altogether many salaried employees.

Now let's talk about the positive side of this. Let's say you work for my company and I'm offering you an all-expenses-paid trip to the Bahamas. Do you want to go? I bet the answer is yes. There's just one requirement: we are leaving Wednesday and you must be caught up on your week's work by then. Can you do it? I'll go out on a limb and guess you said you can. Very good; I'll make the travel arrangements. But before I do, let me ask how you can get caught up on forty hours of work in half the time. The answer is that you will simply choose to get caught up. You will choose to be more efficient and less distracted, and maximize your effort in order to meet the deadline.

Do you do your best work when you feel good or when you feel bad? Do you do great work when someone tells you to do it or when it's your idea? Again, I bet you said, "When I feel good," and "When it's my idea." Your employer cannot mandate such a choice nor demand it. It occurs organically.

What's the message I am trying to convey? A WorkJockey must be responsible, be held accountable, and be given the proper authority to choose to get their job done. Only then can they truly produce a better product or deliver higher performance. We all work best when it's our choice to do so and the incentives are in our favor. The old witticism *What's in it for me?* still applies.

You may not have a choice about transforming your work life right now. You can, however, begin to define your next steps. If you don't start thinking, planning, and acting now, it will never happen. The world will not give you what you want if you don't know what you want or can't articulate your desires clearly. Some folks want more money, some more time off, some a title, some a career, some a job they consider a passion. What do you want? Be specific!

The first time you think about making changes in your work life can be a little challenging. Most of us go to work, do our jobs, go home, and do it all over again the next day without any thought that we could make a change and achieve something better. As a result, nothing changes and we never get ahead unless by accident, and even then the transformation is incremental at best. Take the leaps and bounds necessary to get where and what you want.

Steps you can take:

- Relentlessly analyze your schedule.
- Determine what you can eliminate.
- Determine what you can do to reduce your work load and time at work.
- Schedule your personal time as your priority over work time.
- Work the minimum required hours.
- Use a calendar to plan your personal time.

Be Relentless

To truly pursue the WorkJockey dream you must be relentless. Eat with your mission, sleep with your mission, and become your mission. A WorkJockey uses all the resources and talents at their disposal. You have many more talents than you realize. Take an inventory of them, and if there are deficits, fill them. Surround yourself with like-minded WorkJockeys, and enlighten them in regard to what that means. Help them identify what a WorkJockey is and why it's important to be one. If they meet the definition, they're WorkJockeys. Share their momentum and they can share yours.

Bring the WorkJockeys you know along for the ride. They may have different overall goals and dreams, but the common denominator is always *working less, living more, accomplishing more, and being happy.* How much fun would it be to go on vacation alone? A few might like to, but most recognize that we want and need to take others along with us. We are human, and our nature is togetherness.

Life's meaning is not all about us; it's about others, too. Consider family, friends, colleagues, and co-workers, and include them. By improving the quality of life for others we in turn improve our own quality of life. WorkJockeys also believe it's important to help others develop and to carry them forward with us as we grow and develop. There is strength in numbers and strength in surrounding ourselves with other positive minds. Many brittle twigs banded together become an unbreakable bundle, and it's the same with us.

Adversities

A WorkJockey faces many adversities, but each one garners strength. From the time you were born your body has been exposed to many illnesses and diseases. Your immune system helped you avoid many of those illnesses. Likewise you face many naysayers, and you know it's important to rely on your "immune system" to fight them off.

A WorkJockey is a true leader. But before you can lead others, you must be able to lead yourself. Learn how to manage yourself and your circumstances. Although you cannot control everything around you and how it impacts you, you can control your thoughts. Take control of your thoughts and follow logic before letting your emotions take charge. Your emotions can overwhelm you unless you have prepared in advance for adverse situations and conditions. Why do we plan for disasters such as tornados and hurricanes? Obviously there is no way to know exactly what will happen, but we take steps to avoid danger and mitigate hardship by having extra water and medical supplies on hand.

A WorkJockey prepares for likely distractions and attacks. You zealously guard your time and resources. Time is not unlimited, and neither are resources. With proper planning you can handle every situation effectively by:

- Perpetually working on yourself and your talents
- Remaining moral, ethical, and legal
- Apologizing for mistakes and moving forward
- Remembering that work is not your whole life
- Using work as a tool to get what you want

CHAPTER 12

THE MIND, BODY, AND SPIRIT OF A WORKJOCKEY

You are more than just a worker. You have a mind, body, and spirit. All three components influence your success and happiness. To create the work and life you want, pay attention to your mind, body, and spirit.

A computer programmer knows without question that programming a computer is critical to its successful operation. In the same way, when it comes to your body and your mind, if you put garbage in, you get garbage out, as the saying goes. Zig Ziglar would say, "If you put the good stuff in, you'll get the good stuff out.

The Mind

Managing your thoughts is a major challenge in becoming a WorkJockey. Take inventory of what you're feeding your mind on a daily basis. Everything must be evaluated. Every input into your thoughts has a positive or a negative effect on you.

Unfortunately the scale does not tip easily in your favor – the same level of negative does not equal the same level of positive. You have to push as much negative away as possible by feeding your thoughts positive stimuli. From media to music to interactions with others, everything has an effect on you and you are not immune to it. It is part of being a human. Conscious as well as subconscious stimuli either help you succeed or help you fail. Make conscious decisions about the stimuli you expose yourself to.

When we are born, we are blank slates. The stimuli in our environments shape us and color our perceptions of the world. Our understanding can be accurate or inaccurate. Think of the phrase *Perception is the reality in the eye of the beholder*. Facts become whatever we believe is true. We are not happy when others challenge our beliefs outright because we feel stupid based on our own perceptions.

Knowing that perceptions can be inaccurate, a WorkJockey learns to keep an open mind and seek facts. Facts can change your mind and ultimately change your perception of reality. Seek to educate yourself at all times. Like truth, education stands on its own, and it often stands alone. The truth is not always easy to hear. We prefer to believe what we have always believed, or at least what the majority believe is true.

Everything about you begins with your mind, which is primarily focused on the logical and the transparent – concepts that are simple to grasp or that some might call common sense. I take issue with the term *common sense*. I truly believe that common sense isn't all that common anymore. It has now become *uncommon common sense*. It has been overwritten in many cases by emotion or lack of emotional intelligence.

The mind is the gateway. You think and therefore you become. See yourself having achieved your goals in order to understand what it will feel like to have achieved them and in order to map the route to achieve them. Stephen Covey said, "Begin with the end in mind." It's like taking a vacation; you wouldn't start to travel without answering a few questions like "Where am I going and how do I plan to get there?" It's natural to think in these terms when traveling, but we usually don't think like that when preparing a list of goals.

Some years ago I traveled to Pennsylvania for a speaking engagement. I arrived at the airport and assumed I would catch a cab to my final destination. When I asked the driver what the fee would be to my destination, he said, "Get in and we will figure it out." Finally, after much discussion about why he could not give me a firm price, I found out that my destination was a hundred miles away from the airport! I had no idea that was the case and had not planned appropriately. I learned an important lesson for the future: Know where you're going, and even more important, know how you plan to get there. (Knowing the distance can be helpful, too!) Envision what you want, how you expect to get it, and what information and inspiration you need to make it happen. All those decisions are the work of the mind.

The Body

The body is a peculiar structure. It is very complex, yet mostly a simple organism: you feed it and it continues to function. What you feed it determines how well it functions. If you were to feed your body unhealthy food, illness, disease, and malfunction could result. However, feed it proper nutrition, and your body survives, functions, and thrives.

In addition to feeding your body properly, exercise and challenge it physically. When you go to a gym for the first time and try to lift weights, you will not be very strong. You have to begin with light weights based on your current level of strength. Over time you become stronger and your body responds to the strength-building stimulus. If you miss a few workouts or a few months of workouts, your body loses some strength, but not all the strength you gained over time. So feed your body well, and create positive stress for your body through exercise.

The Spirit

You might not be using your human spirit to its full potential. I know I am not using mine to its full potential even as I write this book. Without getting into a religious discussion, I'm saying that we all know what is wrong and what is right. We can ignore the facts, but we cannot change the facts. Facts are pesky little things; they are persistent devils at revealing the truth. When you put together your WorkJockey plan, stop and ask yourself how you feel about it. Are the goals good for all concerned? If your actions will hurt others, they are likely the wrong actions.

When I ask a group of people how many are good people, most raise their hand. When I ask the same group if they always do the right thing, the hands go down. We are all flawed individuals with much work to be done. That's okay – that, too, is part of being human.

To be a truly happy person, work even harder at doing the right things. The only way to do this is through questioning your spirit and determining whether you seek to harm or help others. This question is at the core of your spiritual development whether you are religious or not. You have an inner compass. If you listen to it, you will live an ethical and true life that helps you get what you want without harming anyone else.

You know the difference between good and bad in your spirit. Zig Ziglar taught me that I must *be the right person and do the right things in order to have the things I want.* Paying attention to your spirit helps you do that.

Take time to breathe, think, evaluate, and respond rather than just react to things that happen, and you will notice immediate and long-term improvements in your life and the lives of those around you whom you might influence.

Here are a few more tips to help you maintain your mind, body, and spirit:

- Read voraciously.
- Maintain a positive mental attitude.
- Look for the good.
- Eat healthy, fresh foods daily.
- Prepare for your mind to challenge you.
- Take inventory of what you feed your mind.
- Perception becomes your reality.
- Educate yourself or someone else will.
- Truth and good ideas stand on their own.
- Spiritual practices and time in nature can soothe your stress.

CHAPTER 13

YOUR HEALTH SUPPORTS YOUR SUCCESS

You must be active before you can acquire.

In the last chapter you read about the importance of your mind, body, and spirit. Becoming a WorkJockey requires a strong focus on your health and physical well-being. After all, what good is all the money and success in the world if you are unhealthy and can't enjoy the fruits of your labor?

Mental, Physical, and Spiritual Health

Mental health is seeing the world in proper perspective – not as being either good or bad, but from the ideal that we are all created equal yet we have different experiences that mold our thinking and our opinions. Right or wrong, this is the reality. You might be a positive person; your glass is always half full. Or you might be a negative person; your glass is always half empty – but if so, you probably decided to put this book down a long time ago. I hope you feel compelled to continue, because either way I believe your outlook will improve. Remember, you can always refill the glass.

Is there any real benefit in looking for the negative in everything? I think this perception is a total waste of thinking. Thinking positively helps you find solutions to problems and celebrate your successes. Dale Carnegie wrote a book entitled *How to Stop Worrying and Start Living*. He writes that worrying about things you have no control over is a waste of your valuable time. I agree. Instead of worrying, get busy making things happen instead of letting things happen to you.

Many books tout the importance of having a positive mental attitude. Finding the positive in every situation or circumstance creates a *solutions mindset*. Thinking negatively bogs you down and makes it difficult to move forward, and sometimes even impossible. The next time you feel negative thoughts creeping into your mind, remember that approximately 80 percent of the things you worry over you can't do anything about. And the 20 percent you can do something about, you should take action on as soon as you determine a solution.

In regard to physical health, I don't mean having a runner's body, a weightlifter's strength, or a bodybuilder's physique; I mean maintaining a healthy body, or being as healthy as you can from today forward. You and only you can make the decision to be healthier. It can seem overwhelming to make the changes necessary to become reasonably healthy. I understand that because I was there once.

Maybe you only need to add a little exercise, eat a little less, refrain from too much alcohol, or limit or eliminate tobacco. Whatever the need, you have all the tools necessary to make the changes. Think in terms of moderation at the very least, and elimination of unhealthy habits at best. You know what you must do even if you don't know exactly how to do it. Help is out there and you don't have to reinvent the wheel. Everything you wish to change or improve has been done before and there are formulas everywhere to help you succeed. The hardest part is taking the first step.

Be prepared to fall off the wagon a few times (or many) before your transformation is permanent. That's okay. Your focus is on a lifestyle change and not a temporary behavioral shift. After a while you will wonder why it took you so long to see the light.

If you have to make major changes to improve your health, it might be nearly impossible to prevent a relapse, so it might take longer than you envision. But with each longer period of time between relapses you are making progress. Don't be discouraged. Whether you want to quit alcohol or drugs, or need to start a regular exercise program, if you begin you will make progress and succeed.

It has been weird for me to see bodybuilders, for example, with the drive and tenacity to diet to the extreme to get to their competitive weight and health level, only to see them smoking tobacco or marijuana or ingesting cocaine. It just doesn't make sense. If you tend to become addicted to such things, or even to something like caffeine or sugar, you might need professional counseling beyond advice and coaching. If you need to make a major health change, talk with your physician or another professional who can give you the support you need. You don't have to make changes alone – unless you thrive on working by yourself. WorkJockeys know that asking for help is a sign of strength.

I promise not to preach to you, but let's talk about spiritual health. I'm not in church every time the doors are open; however,

I do believe in God. I have a little chitchat with Him nightly. In my opinion there are just too many examples of the presence of a higher power to not believe there is one.

What would the world be like if everyone believed that we all answer to a higher power? When we do not treat all mankind with kindness and respect we pay a very high price in the end. We have all seen what some describe as karma. I think what happens to or for you is what you manifest. In short, you reap what you sow. Sometimes you don't correlate the two, so you fail to learn from your mistakes.

I am learning to be a better person today than I was yesterday. This is a tall order, I know, because we're not all taught this. To realize the benefits of following this path, just begin now, from wherever you are. Everyone would like to identify themselves as a good person. I know because I have asked about this many times in my leadership classes. Our intentions are not visible; only our actions are visible. Do your actions reveal you as a good person? What would your friends, relatives, and acquaintances say about you? What impressions do you leave behind with those you meet?

Give Change Some Time

As I wrote earlier, when I decided to lose weight I knew it would not happen overnight, but I knew the results were worth waiting for and that little successes along the way would encourage me to continue. Things like comments from friends: "Sam, are you losing weight; are you getting skinny?" And when I was taken off cholesterol medicine and found my blood pressure normal. And later when I began to see an athletic pulse below forty-five. These were all worth waiting for. A more profound feeling was, first, physical health, then feeling better inside and outside, with greater self-esteem. I gained confidence that I not only could lose the weight and get healthy, I could in fact maintain this change indefinitely by making it a lifestyle change and, for me, a paradigm shift.

Even now I am haunted by old behaviors taught to me in grade school and at home to eat everything on my oversized plate. It is important to understand that your mind must change before your behavior can follow. Changing your mind changes everything. If there is one thing I have learned that will help you move forward it is to get rid of "stinkin' thinkin'." Thinking in a negative way leads you away from your personal goals and into the path of disaster. Many people think that everything and everyone is against them, and of course this is not true; most folks don't care about you or your existence. So don't live for them. Live for yourself first, and family and real friends second. Become the kind of human being you are proud of and then help others reach their goals. *We need many more good people in the world; be one of them.*

Napoleon Hill describes things this way: "Every adversity... carries with it a seed of an equal or greater benefit." It took me a while to understand this. For example, my friend Lou Ann Montgomery's house was damaged terribly during a violent storm. It destroyed the front of her house. Lou Ann and I served on the Bay County Domestic Violence Task Force board together, and met monthly. I mentioned Hill's concept to her and asked if she could see something good happening as a result. Because of all the emotions of her loss, I believe she might have been upset with me. We are friends, so she never let it show. I asked her the same question over several months and she replied no. Finally

I decided it was time to let it rest for a while. Nearly six months passed and I asked again, and before I could get the words out of my mouth she said yes, finally she could see it: she got a new great room in place of the room that was destroyed. She said further that this would not have happened if the storm had not caused the damage.

Since then I have looked closely at events and I'm convinced Hill's premise is true. Even if you take the negative side and say it can't be true, wouldn't it be better emotionally and spiritually to believe in the positive? It would reduce much heartache, and you would always see the glass as half full. This can be your paradigm shift. You, too, can be looking for Napoleon Hill's seed of an equivalent benefit in every adversity.

If you think back over your lifetime you can probably find the seeds of equivalent benefits in bad things that happened to you. Sometimes you think you know what's good for you and sometimes you dodge a bullet when you don't get what you ask for – the result you were seeking was not the right one for you. Once I applied for a director's job at a non-profit. Someone else got the position. It turned out that not only was she better suited for the position, it was not a good fit for me in the long run. Wow – maybe I dodged that bullet.

Other times I sought opportunities and it was like they were dropped into my lap. I don't believe in coincidence. I believe things happen for a reason. And I also believe our efforts put these things in motion and build sufficient momentum to take us where we want to go. *Seek and you shall find* is a great motto to remember. Keep on thinking and focusing on your end goals. In time opportunities will present themselves as long as you don't take your eyes off the prize. Keep your eyes and your mind open and focused.

Ten things to remember:

- Focus on mental and physical health.
- Focus on the positive.
- Stop worrying about what you cannot change.
- Maintain a positive mental attitude.
- Maintain fitness and wellness.
- Make a paradigm shift – think differently.
- Remember that someone is always watching.
- Constant improvement and maintenance are necessary for a rewarding life.
- Overnight success does *not* exist.
- Unanswered prayers may be one of God's greatest gifts.

Before trying to work on your job,
begin by working on yourself.

CHAPTER 14

WORKJOCKEYS LEAD

Influence

It is said that leadership is about influence. I say there's a little more to it. My proposed definition of leadership comes from the premise that leadership is about the morals, ethics, and values you use, intentionally or unintentionally, to influence the behavior of others to create higher performance, results, and success. That's good leadership as opposed to bad or ugly leadership. Help people avoid influences from others that take them off track, and create your own ability to influence others in your work.

Influence can be a dangerous factor, because the minute we start showing who we are and what we're about, we begin to influence people... good, bad, or indifferent. Lots of people have influence, but they can be bad people. ISIS is a good example, and the terrorist stuff that's going on in the world right now. Terrorists have tremendous influence on the people they recruit. Good people have influence. Bad people have influence.

Don't lose track of where you're going. One illustration of this happened to me when I was twenty-six and working as an investigator. I was trying to improve things. Captain Danny Boyle, whom I respected very much, came to me one day and said, "We don't need you improving things around here. Just go do your freaking job and put somebody in jail." (Of course, he used a different word.)

At the time I thought, "Man, what's wrong with me? Am I not doing what these guys want me to do?" Later I realized that in the private sector they'd write me a check for that kind of stuff. It's called consulting.

But in government, it wasn't well respected or accepted. So I was being influenced a little bit. Now, I did create a tight base. What I mean by that is I created a protective shield – and after twenty-four years I was not jaded. I didn't hate people. I wasn't headed to the grave, and I wasn't an alcoholic. A lot of those guys were those things because they hadn't flushed the positives into their minds. And I think that's what hurts a lot of people.

Use influence to reach your goals, not others' goals. Don't try to live up to others' expectations. I expect more of myself than I do from others, and I expect more *from* myself than I do from others, so therefore I'm going to do better for myself than I do for others. And if others are not so inclined, that's okay too.

Shield of Protection

Create your own "shield of protection" so that the culture, the environment, your supervisor, and your co-workers do not influence you negatively.

It's an uphill battle to do what I'm proposing, and that's why it's critical to take charge of yourself first before you can expect your organization to do anything for you. And there's a good chance the organization won't do anything; it'll be totally up to you.

The same thing applies to being a manager. We talk about leading employees. If you try to wing it with employees, you're going to fall on your face – it's just not going to go well. People accept mistakes, but if you're constantly stepping on yourself, it's not going to go well.

Managers can feel like they're too vulnerable to admit mistakes, and just pretend that they didn't do it or it was somebody else's fault. That deteriorates the trust that their employees have in them. It's like punching holes in a bucket; the water pours right out. Whatever good will they had is gone. It's like a sports coach who says, "If we win, you guys did it. If we lose, I did it." He doesn't just say it. He means it.

Umbrella Management

Managers are there to take care of the people they represent. It's almost like a politician who represents a city or a state. If they're not looking out for their constituency – the people who report to them – they ought to be fired. They should take care of their staff while meeting organizational goals.

If you're a manager and bad news comes that doesn't involve those who report to you directly, you should keep that news off their backs. Avoid the concept of misery loving company. If your supervisor chews you out and then you chew out your own troops, sharing your anger and frustration, all you're doing is interfering with their performance. They need to be firing on all cylinders. They can't do it if you're distracting them. And their distraction is likely to lead to your demise.

It's the same when Mom and Dad come home and let their kids see their frustrations and their disagreements, whether work-related or personal. The kids need to be focused on school. They need to be focused on moving forward. If their parents are having problems – and everybody has them – being exposed to them distracts them and they can't perform well in school.

Be an *umbrella manager*. Keep that crap from rolling downhill and keep it off your people. Keep things moving along without distracting your staff.

Managers can overreact to something, destroying the morale of their troops, and yet it really has no immediate impact on the manager. But it will later because they're letting it travel right on down, and eventually it will rise back up.

When things are going really well and a manager gets some praise from the top, that's the time to close the umbrella, step out of the way, and let that praise flow down to the folks below. That's a true umbrella manager.

CHAPTER 15

CONTINUING YOUR PROGRESS

Now that you have joined the WorkJockey club, how will you maintain your membership? Guard this new philosophy and lifestyle against all distractions, interruptions, and roadblocks that try to derail you. There will be many that will try to blow up your affiliation with this unique club. Club membership is small – very few folks ever commit to this club.

Many people will be jealous of your efforts to take complete control of your work and life. Forget the mantra of work/life balance. Remember, you work to live rather than live to work. You are like a salmon that swims upstream; only other WorkJockeys know why you do it and why your very survival is dependent on it. Be obsessive in this endeavor. You will be the odd man or woman out of the crowd. It's easy to follow the river's flow to where everyone else is going or has already been. But you don't want to be just another drop of water in the river.

Develop new habits and stick to them until they become subconscious behaviors. You will come to believe this to be the norm even if you appear to be the only one moving in this new direction. It will be uncomfortable for a time, but later it will feel as though you were behaving this way your entire life. Think of it like your first time driving a car, if you can remember that far back. You were alert to everything around you and yet you followed the same path as everyone else. With the WorkJockey mindset you eventually wonder why everyone else is not going in your direction. This will take a little getting used to, but you will get used to it.

Remember when you were learning to swim? Everything was scary. But when you finally learned to swim you could do it almost effortlessly. I am not saying everything will be effortless, but the effort is worth it for your future.

When you use or think of the word *WorkJockey*, you will wonder why no one thought of it before now. Those who have to work to live – and that is most of us – should learn to jockey our work lives to better suit our intended lives. It should not be the other way around; yet we have been taught that it is the other way around since our very first job. "You should be happy to have a job. A paycheck is thanks enough for your work." Poppycock!

We need meaning, reason, and reward in our work far beyond a paycheck. To maintain high-performance work requires engagement in the process. How do you get employee engagement? By employing the notion that work must have meaning for employees beyond income. If it does not mean more than a paycheck, employees deliver mediocre results at best.

Being a WorkJockey is not only good for employees, it's also good for employers. The mindset and behaviors are win-wins for both. When employees have their needs met financially and emotionally, they work more effectively.

All employees want some basic things. They want enough income to pay their bills and feed their families. They want to be appreciated and rewarded for the work they do. They want to be valued as human beings and as productive members of their organization. The way to get there from where they are now is for their employer to realize they are working for their own benefit first and foremost, and not their employer's. They are willing to do a good and even a great job once they are shown appreciation. Keep in mind that this begins with the end result in mind. It occurs after the employee's needs are met. I digress a moment to present this concept because I know employees, supervisors, and heads of organizations should recognize what's in it for them if they embrace the WorkJockey philosophy.

Employees with the WorkJockey mindset understand why they work. They place work, and time for work, in a box. They work outside this box to determine how they will conduct their lives, then they merge the two. Like Legos, or a puzzle, you cannot successfully put together pieces that don't match or are not meant to be together. If you force them together, your efforts will be unsuccessful.

I put together an entertainment center once. I was very excited because I had not been known for being particularly handy at building things. I had used a manual screwdriver to put it together, and my hand was killing me. My muscles were sore and my hand was red. Yet when I was down to the final piece, I was thinking it was worth it – and then I could not connect the final piece. Nothing I tried worked, and finally I took a break to regroup. I decided to take a look at the diagram and the instructions. Much to my displeasure, I had put everything together backwards, so it was never going to work. I realized I had to dismantle it and start over. Did I mention my hand was killing me? I did not feel I had the strength to do it again. But I am not one to quit. I ran, or rather drove to the local hardware store and bought an electric screwdriver. I grudgingly reviewed the instructions, dismantled it, and put it together the right way. Wow, what a learning experience that was. I don't want to do that again.

The moral to my story is don't reinvent the wheel, as I've mentioned earlier once or twice. Follow a proven path. If there is no proven path, take a little time and plan your steps well before you hurt your hand trying to manipulate an outcome, put something together backwards, and then have to start over.

Continue to Evaluate Your Needs

You looked at your needs early on in the WorkJockey process. It's always important to ask yourself these questions periodically to ensure you are happy with your journey:

- How much money is needed for paying my bills and feeding my family?
- How much time do I have to devote to work?
- How much time do I wish to devote to work if it were up to me?
- What do I want to accomplish in the end?
- What will be my legacy?

Keep in mind that these questions have very different answers for each individual, and they might have very different answers for you at different stages of your life. Our goals change, our needs change, and our circumstances change.

The answers to these questions are alive. They grow and develop over time. Your current answer to the first question might be "I need $50,000 to meet my current needs." Stop right there. This is make or break time. If you do not currently earn this amount, this is the first item to rectify before developing further as a WorkJockey. Find and acquire employment that will provide this income. For the sake of discussion, let's say you already earn this income. This is a good beginning.

Your current answer to the second question might be "I devote fifty-plus hours a week to my work." Again, stop there and determine how you might either reduce your hours and live on less income or obtain a better position or promotion that will net you the needed income to level the field.

Your answer to the third question might be "I wish to devote only forty hours per week maximum to my work." If so, you have some explaining to do to prove you can do the same job, or even a better job, or produce a better product, with more effort and fewer hours. You would have to work smarter and more efficiently.

Your answer to the fourth question might be "What is the end? Is it the end of my work life – the end of my career, or is it the end of my life?" Determine whether you are in a job, a career, or a passion. A job pays the bills and feeds your family. A career pays the bills, feeds your family, and makes you part of something larger than yourself. You have a purpose in this work. And it could be that your work is a passion. A passion is something that pays your bills, feeds your family, makes you part of something larger than yourself, *and* is something you would do for free if money were no object for you.

Your answer to the fifth question might be "My legacy will be saving lives, helping lives, making folks' lives better, raising children, and helping others." Whatever it is, it will be your legacy. You wish to be remembered for this.

The idea that we can *work less, live more, accomplish more, and be happy* is real. It's not easy to do, but you can do it. You have to challenge the status quo. You have to learn to win friends and influence people, as Dale Carnegie would say. This requires the cooperation of others. You cannot go it alone. Be clear about where you're going and how you plan to get there. Learn when to be flexible in order to create this new opportunity, this new way of thinking. You don't want others shutting you down while you're signing up for WorkJockey membership. And you certainly don't want others to extinguish your new WorkJockey life. You want others to embrace it, and perhaps you will even set up a new culture in which others will participate.

I wrote earlier that the WorkJockey culture is good for all concerned. It's a win-win proposition. Once you live up to your part of the bargain, others will find it in their best interests to live up to theirs. *What's in it for me* applies to employers and employees. No one has to lose for any one party to win. I caution you that people will try to stop you. They are the lazy ones who like things the way they have always been, either because they are uncomfortable with change or because the system in place works for them. You will not be able to win them over, so don't waste your time. Be confident, knowing that they are truly in the minority and will not be able to stop you. They are temporary roadblocks that you have to work past to get from where you are to where you want to be. And they might find themselves obsolete in the new culture, and remove themselves.

Keep on keeping on until you can answer the questions above to your satisfaction and begin moving expeditiously to your new life and permanent membership as a WorkJockey.

Take a Close Look

How is your life going? Are you getting what you want out of it? Who is ultimately responsible for your life? By now you have an idea where I'm going with these questions... you are the one ultimately responsible for living your life successfully.

Sit down right now and decide where you are going and how you plan to get there. Take out a spiral notebook, or better yet go to an office supply store and purchase a project planner, and write down your thoughts and ideas daily. Record the date and time and maybe even where you were when you received the thought or idea. This information could be very important to you in the future. Whether you act consciously on every idea is not that important; your subconscious will begin working toward your ideas and goals even if you don't do anything concrete right now.

You'll never again be where you are today, so what are you waiting for? Time is not on your side, and it is not limitless. It's up to each one of us to decide if we are willing to do what others don't and put our train on the right track. Doing the things that others are not willing to do is what makes some people more successful than others. This is what champions are made of. This is what makes Olympic athletes gold medalists. I coined a term, The Theory of No Competition™, because you are not really competing with anyone else; you are only competing with yourself. What are you willing to do to reach your goals? Whatever it is you want, step up and get it.

Once while coaching a young baseball player, I noticed he continually walked up to the plate and watched as strike after strike crossed the plate. Sometimes he would get a walk, but more often he would strike out having never swung the bat. When he was headed to the plate one time I told him to leave the bat at the dugout. He argued for a moment but I insisted. He walked up to the plate, embarrassed, but aware he was now helpless at the plate. Strike after strike passed the plate, and he struck out. He came back from the plate upset and crying. I told him he didn't need the bat if he wasn't going to use it. I also told him that even if he were to strike out, he had a better chance of getting a hit if he would swing rather than just stand there. Later, when he was at bat again, he swung the bat and hit the ball.

Be willing to step up and swing from the plate, and be even more determined to get the hit you came for. More professional players strike out than get a hit, but when they get a hit or a home run it can be a historic event. When has a batter ever received a standing ovation or had their team waiting at the plate to congratulate them for getting a walk? Only those who are willing to step up to the plate and swing for the hit they came for can share these moments. Don't wait another minute – another second. Start getting what you want from life right now.

CHAPTER 16

WHEN YOU FALL OFF TRACK

Don't let an incident change your positive personality and mentality.

When trying to make a point, sometimes a single thought escapes me. I'll ask the person I'm speaking with to wait a moment so I can reclaim my train of thought. Moments later I'm able to recall the thought and continue.

Thoughts, like trains, travel on tracks, but sometimes they jump the track. And when you speak to people, sometimes they're not traveling on your track. Your message can be easily lost or misunderstood. Communication is statistically the number one problem in every organization. But did you know that it is the number one solvable problem as well?

There are things you can do to communicate more effectively with others. Talk to others directly and simply, and then ask questions to determine if your message has been communicated as intended. Are you communicating a message that is being understood? Learn to locate your train and maintain the track so you don't derail during a conversation. Determine what it is you want to accomplish by sharing your message, and create strategies for reaching those goals.

In addition to removing old habits and teaching yourself new skills, learn how to bypass, eliminate, and downright avoid triggers that send you plummeting off the track. Something put you where you were before you made the conscious decision to become a WorkJockey. Such temptations might still be lingering in your consciousness. Maintain your new behavior until it becomes a habit and finally embeds itself into your subconscious. Even when your subconscious is working for you and not against you, temptation, distraction, and even friends and relatives can throw you off your new game. They can do this intentionally or unintentionally, but the results are the same. You become a train off the track.

Your path will grow cold and can even grow weeds if you don't travel your track regularly. The good news is that it's easier to get back on track than to try to find a new one. When you began making changes toward your goal of becoming a WorkJockey, it was much harder. You had to learn how, and then take action. If you find yourself off track, you now know what to do.

Take action sooner rather than later. The longer you stay off track, the less likely you are to get back on track, and even more important, the less likely the track will remain functional or even present so you can return to it. One of the examples I mentioned earlier was weight loss. It takes a little study and work to find a plan that works for you, and you will still need to make adjustments in order to make it optimal for you. Some folks count carbs; others count fat; and still others, like me, focus only on calories. If you don't eat too many calories, fat and carbs may be moot points because you are unlikely to get too much of either if you watch, document, and monitor your calorie intake.

My other example was strength training. You lift light weights, and as you get stronger you find that you can lift heavier weights. But if you miss working out for a few weeks or months, you'll be starting over. The good news is that if you don't wait too long you won't have to start at the very beginning; you can determine what your level of strength has become since you last worked out and begin from that point. The same analogy applies to cardiovascular and endurance workouts.

The moral of these examples is to get started wherever you are, take action, and make progress. Even if you drop off from time to time, progress is about quality, quantity, and consistency. You maintain progress by remaining in action mode more often than not. I know you have heard this before: it requires a lifestyle change; a shift. I call it a paradigm shift.

Being a WorkJockey is different for each person because we are all different. You are unique. The way you pursue being a WorkJockey will be different from mine even though the results you seek might be similar. You can compare notes and learn from others who have been successful – and from those who failed. There is no sense wasting your time. Learn the fastest, most direct path to follow for you. Don't let anyone tell you there is only one way to be a WorkJockey. Until they read this book or attend one of my presentations they don't know what a WorkJockey is anyway, much less what it takes to become one. You have a leg up on them if you get moving now.

Your family, if you have one at this time, can be either helpful or a hindrance. Statistics indicate they will be all-in to support you. This is not like the support required for a workaholic. Being a WorkJockey is good for the family, and your family will recognize this. Many people work too much, and no one in the family wants to support that unless the extra work brings in extra money that the family desperately needs. You are unlikely to enjoy any luxuries that your extra work might finance because you're working too darn much.

It's okay to make mistakes as long as you learn something from them.

Tips to remember:

- Risk and reward happens.
- To change you have to truly commit to the change.
- Work is a tool.
- WorkJockeys have to maintain their WorkJockey track.
- Work toward fewer injuries and less illness.
- Work toward greater engagement at work.

CHAPTER 17

YOUR WORKJOCKEY LEGACY

Let go of the past so you can live in your future.

What would the world be like without you? Who has influenced you, and more important, who is influencing you now? People leave permanent imprints on you throughout your life. And you leave imprints on others as well.

You begin creating your legacy when you are born. Day in and day out you are in contact with many people. I read an article from an embroidery company that stated that an emblem embroidered on your shirt is likely to be seen by 346 people in one business day. You want to make a good impression. You leave some form of impression on others no matter what you do, often in only moments.

Leaving a legacy takes longer than a moment, of course, and can last for generations. It requires constant work on your part. Most agree that life is worth living, but might not agree that we live our lives for the benefit of and in service to others. This can occur actively or passively, but it does occur.

There is no requirement that you be wealthy to leave a legacy. There will always be those who have more and a majority who have less.

You touch and reach people in significant ways, but you rarely hear about them. Investigating this premise illuminates a new mindset: your legacy is occurring with or without your conscious intention. You've heard of those trying to get their fifteen minutes of fame... a legacy requires a lifetime to create. Moments build upon moments, years upon years, and one day your story is complete. You have an obligation as one who has had more than most. Your ability to simply read and understand this book is certainly a blessing, and an ability that many in this world do not have.

Try to do the right thing. This is more important than doing things correctly. The right thing is always the right thing. It's not always easy to do the right thing. You might even get beaten up while trying to do the right thing. You might be in the minority when trying to do the right thing. But you know in your heart it's the right thing to do. You might not know until much later, if at all, how important doing the right thing was. It's a gift to see what your work and sacrifice does for others and ultimately how it comes back around to you.

I took a position as chief of police for a small city with a troubled police department. This department needed direction and support, but mostly it needed leadership. Over a period of eleven months I worked with the staff to create a team environment. We created an environment of trust, respect, support, professionalism, and progress. I was tested by some, given ultimatums by others, and yet others seemed to thrive in the developing culture.

During my eleventh month on the job, I was out of town on vacation at Disney World in Orlando and received a call from a staff member. He told me that a city commissioner was calling a special meeting and planned to make a motion for my removal without cause. I prepared myself for the possible outcome and thought about what might have brought this about.

Upon my return, much to my surprise, I found that my staff had rallied to fight my removal. The night of the meeting the commission room was filled with staff members, citizens, and the media. The commissioner made his motion to have me removed. He gave no reasons and said he wanted no discussion about the matter.

Another commissioner stated he would allow those who came to speak to do so. I sat quietly for a moment, observing what was taking place in total disbelief. One by one each member of the department went to the podium to speak on my behalf, giving example after example of why I should remain as chief.

I hadn't reflected on how I handled the day-to-day operations in the department; I simply followed the philosophy of doing what I felt was right and in the best interests of those I was leading. I wasn't always right, but I always tried to do the right thing. This meeting was a humbling experience for me. However, it validated my approach to the responsibilities of the job. Even if I had gotten fired that evening I would have left with my head held high and without regret, knowing I had done what I felt was right and what others also believed was right.

In the end the commissioner not only did not receive a second to his motion, he withdrew his motion. I remained chief of police for four years until being offered a private sector job as chief of field operations for an internet company. I now own and operate a company that conducts employee training, leadership coaching, human resources consulting, and presentations. I work with other companies to promote their missions and instill the values I brought to the chief of police position many years ago.

Each and every one of us impacts many people. Hopefully our legacies will not be forgotten. A world without each of us would not be the same. Leave your own permanent mark on the world. Keep on improving your future and bringing the WorkJockey mindset to the world!

ABOUT THE AUTHOR

Sam Slay, SPHR, SHRM-SCP, spent twenty-four years in law enforcement as an officer, investigator, trainer, administrator, and chief of police, focusing on the power of people and the power of enthusiasm. He was then hired as chief of field operations for a leading wireless internet company and later promoted to vice president of sales and marketing.

Sam focuses on speaking, training, and consulting in the areas of productivity, communication, leadership development, and human resources management. He recognizes the worth of the individual employee's contribution in the workplace and knows that failure to foster their contributions is like waiting for a wrecking ball to dismantle your organization.

Sam's training, coaching, and consulting resources are the culmination of decades of training and consulting experience with companies such as AT&T, Champion International, Clark Equipment, Coach Leatherware, Colgate, Corning, Exxon, Hewlett Packard, Honeywell, IBM, Merck, NASA, Rockwell International, and others.

To learn more about how Sam can help your organization or to book him to speak to your group, visit SamSlay.com.

www.ingramcontent.com/pod-product-compliance
Lightning Source LLC
Chambersburg PA
CBHW052120090426

42741CB00009B/1887